TRAVELLERS

LIBYA

By
THEA MACAULAY

Written by Thea Macaulay
Original photography by Danny Levy Sheehan

Published by Thomas Cook Publishing
A division of Thomas Cook Tour Operations Limited
Company registration no. 3772199 England
The Thomas Cook Business Park, Unit 9, Coningsby Road,
Peterborough PE3 8SB, United Kingdom
Email: books@thomascook.com, Tel: + 44 (0) 1733 416477
www.thomascookpublishing.com

Produced by Cambridge Publishing Management Limited
Burr Elm Court, Main Street, Caldecote CB23 7NU

ISBN: 978-1-84848-191-6

Text © 2009 Thomas Cook Publishing
Maps © 2009 Thomas Cook Publishing/PCGraphics (UK) Limited

Series Editor: Maisie Fitzpatrick
Production/DTP: Steven Collins

Printed and bound in Italy by Printer Trento

Cover photography: Front L–R: © LOOK Die Bildagentur der Fotografen
GmbH/Alamy; © MARKA/Alamy; © Pavan Aldo/SIME/4Corners Images
Back: © Giovanni Simeone/SIME/4Corners Images

All rights reserved. No part of this publication may be reproduced, stored in
a retrieval system or transmitted, in any form or by any means, electronic,
mechanical, recording or otherwise, in any part of the world, without prior
permission of the publisher. Requests for permission should be made to the
publisher at the above address.

Although every care has been taken in compiling this publication, and the
contents are believed to be correct at the time of printing, Thomas Cook Tour
Operations Limited cannot accept any responsibility for errors or omissions,
however caused, or for changes in details given in the guidebook, or for the
consequences of any reliance on the information provided. Descriptions and
assessments are based on the author's views and experiences when writing and
do not necessarily represent those of Thomas Cook Tour Operations Limited.

Contents

Introduction

Libya has many tales to tell, sights to show and a warm welcome to enchant visitors. Yet to much of the outside world this fascinating country remains at best little known and at worst completely misunderstood, a legacy lingering from years of political isolation. Change is in the air, however, and travellers can now enjoy Libya's ancient Mediterranean cities and breathtaking desert landscape in the context of a modern, stable society.

Libya is a Middle Eastern Islamic country, with attractive mosques and labyrinthine old cities, such as the medina (old town) of the cosmopolitan capital, Tripoli. It is also a Mediterranean country, with a palm-lined coast and spectacular examples of ancient ruins. In addition, it is an African country, with vast swathes of the Sahara within its borders, and captivating oasis towns. The country's official name is the Great Socialist People's Libyan Arab Jamahiriya ('Rule of the Masses'), in accordance with the vision of its long-term ruler, Colonel Muammar Qaddafi. In recent years, Colonel Qaddafi has taken significant steps towards improving his country's international relations and has also relaxed his control a little over the lives of its people. The government neither actively promotes nor discourages tourism, and visitor numbers, although growing, remain relatively low. Visa requirements make it necessary for visitors to travel on an escorted tour,

which may feel prescriptive at the time of planning a holiday, but this is an impression easily shaken off once you arrive. Being accompanied by a local guide provides an invaluable opportunity to get to know the country better and can help with everything from orientation to communication.

Libyan society is very family-centred and in many ways faithful to age-old cultural traditions, which are balanced by modern developments. Hospitality is important to Libyans, and visitors are made to feel welcome. The novelty value of tourists has not yet completely worn off and you may well come across people who are delighted to have the opportunity to stop you in the street just for a chat – in the non-intrusive way typical of the Libyan culture.

Libya remains steeped in a history so varied and enthralling that the past is a major feature of most itineraries. Dotted along the Mediterranean coastline is an impressive collection of amazingly well-preserved classical cities dating from ancient Greece, the Roman Empire and even before. Within day-trip distance of Tripoli are two of the most stunning reminders of Roman Libya: the cities of Leptis Magna and Sabratha. The eastern coastal region of Cyrenaica is both geographically and culturally distinct. This greenest part of Libya is home to the ancient Greek cities of Cyrene, Tolmeita and Apollonia, as well as a beautiful collection of Byzantine mosaics in the Qasr Libya museum. Moving from the ancient to the more recent past, Cyrenaica is also the location of an important World War II site at Tobruk.

Then there is the Libyan Sahara, a seemingly endless yet surprisingly diverse landscape of sand and rocks. The desert takes up most of the country and exploring it requires long journeys. It is well worth the effort, however, to experience the ethereal beauty of sculpted sand dunes, bizarre rock formations and oasis lakes. Here too are legacies of ancient civilisations, most notably the impressive prehistoric rock paintings of the Acacus area in the southwest. The people of the Sahara have their own distinctive culture and their world is intriguingly different from that of northern Libya.

An Ubari desert oasis lake with palm trees

The land

Situated in North Africa, Libya is geographically dominated by two things: the Mediterranean Sea, which makes up its northern border, and the Sahara desert, which covers some 95 per cent of its territory. Unsurprisingly, sand is the main feature of the landscape. This huge country (the fourth-biggest on the continent) has six land neighbours. Egypt lies in the east, Tunisia and Algeria to the west, and Niger, Chad and Sudan in the south.

Regions

Historically, Libya was divided into three distinct and separate provinces: Tripolitania in the northwest, Cyrenaica in the east and Fezzan in the south. The country was definitively unified in the 20th century, with the traditional area names remaining in use as the administrative regions. Although Tripolitania and Cyrenaica still cover large areas, in this book the chapters dealing with these regions focus on the coastal stretches, where most of the historical sites are concentrated. To reflect its cultural and geographical distinctiveness, the Jebel Nafusa ('Western Mountains') region has been separated from Tripolitania into a different chapter.

Coast

Libya's coastline is 1,770km (1,100 miles) long and follows an almost horseshoe-shaped path, with the Gulf of Sirt in the middle. In western Tripolitania the coastal Sahel al-Jefara (Jefara Plain) leads inland to the Jebel Nafusa range of hills, which were once volcanic. The greenest part of Libya is the northeast, where the Jebel al-Akhdar ('Green Mountains') of Cyrenaica soar sharply from sea level to an elevation of about 600m (1,970ft). The coastline itself features long stretches of white and yellow sand, broken by pockets where rocky cliffs descend straight into the sea and secluded coves emerge.

Desert

The Libyan Sahara is a tapestry of sand and rock, the fabric of which varies immensely over vast distances. Among its most distinctive and interesting features are *idehan* (sand-seas) of towering dunes, salt-water oasis lakes and basalt mountain ranges, such as the Jebel Acacus in the southwest. Sand-seas are the most iconic of the desert landscapes, but much of the Libyan Sahara actually consists of *hamada* (gravelly plateaux). The desert is

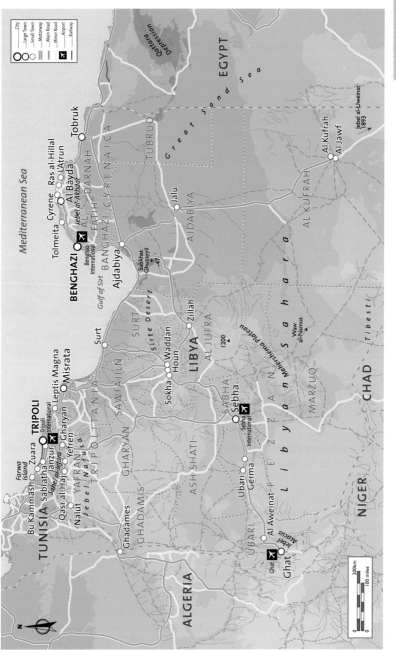

Green Mountain at Ras al-Hillal

nothing if not evocative. The never-ending sand dunes are like a dreamscape. In the mountainous regions, bizarrely shaped rocks seem like sculptures. Elsewhere, dark gravelly plains create an almost Martian impression. Libya has no permanent rivers, although there are *wadis*, dry riverbeds which very occasionally flood. The Tibesti mountain range in the far south is Libya's highest ground.

Flora and fauna

The flora of the coast is characteristically Mediterranean. Palm, eucalyptus, olive and citrus trees grow alongside flowering plants such as oleander and bougainvillea. Many of these were planted by the Italians during their relatively brief occupation. The Jebel al-Akhdar mountains are surprisingly thickly forested, with juniper and pine trees clinging to the slopes, although this wooded region makes up just a tiny percentage of Libyan land. Date palms are the icons of the oases, while elsewhere in the desert acacia trees and salt grasses are commonly the only vegetation around.

Wildlife is limited throughout Libya. The most visible creatures are lizards and migratory birds. A number of other animals, from snakes and small rodents to fennec foxes, waddan (mountain sheep) and gazelles, hide themselves in the wilds of the Sahara. The mammal species are most numerous in the remote southeast and southwest of the country. More information on Saharan wildlife is provided in the feature 'Desert ecosystem' (*see pp118–19*).

Environment and sustainability

Only a very small proportion of Libyan land, mainly in the coastal regions, is suitable for agriculture. Palm trees, including date palms, are one of the few crops that are widely cultivated. Water is the foremost environmental concern and the Great Man-Made River project (*see box*) was set up to deal with this. As an oil-producing nation, Libya is fossil-fuel dependent. Environmental

THE GREAT MAN-MADE RIVER

Modern Libya is a hive of development activity and the biggest project by far is the Great Man-Made River (GMR), pitched by Colonel Qaddafi as the 'Eighth Wonder of the World'. Massive pipelines were built to siphon and carry water from the underground basins of the Libyan Sahara to the cities. Tripoli and Benghazi are among the cities already supplied by the GMR and work continues to extend the project. Although it has proven an effective solution so far, the GMR has been the source of much debate. The capacity of the basins is not infinite and there are concerns about the effect on the fragile desert environment.

conservation does not appear to be at the top of the government's agenda. There is a particularly big problem with rubbish disposal, and litter unfortunately blights many areas just outside towns.

The Ubari Sand Sea after a rare burst of rain

History

10,000–2000 BC	Neolithic period. Nomadic peoples inhabit the Sahara, which was once green and fertile. Early rock paintings are created.
c. **900 BC**	The indigenous Garamantes Empire is established in southern Libya and flourishes until AD 500 when underground water supplies run dry.
c. **700 BC**	Seafaring Phoenicians establish Lebdah (Leptis Magna). The cities of Oea (Tripoli) and Sabratha follow and all are inhabited by Punic settlers, North Africans of Phoenician origin.
631 BC	Cyrene is founded by Greek migrants from Thera (Santorini). Cyrenaica (northeastern Libya) develops into an important colony for Greece.
146 BC	After several wars with Rome, the Punic civilisation is defeated. Tripolitania (northwestern Libya) is briefly ruled by the Numidians and then by the Romans.
96 BC	Greece formally gives up Cyrenaica to Rome. Tripolitania and Cyrenaica are unified under Roman rule and both provinces thrive. The Garamantes remain unconquered and become trading partners with the Romans.
AD 365	A massive earthquake devastates coastal cities.
431	The Vandals (a Germanic tribe) seize Tripolitania.
533	Libya is conquered by the Byzantines.
642–63	Arab soldiers take control of the country, spreading Islam. The Berber tribes continue to defend their traditions and there are numerous uprisings.
8th–16th centuries	Libya is fought over by various dynasties and controlled from Damascus, Baghdad, Cairo and Morocco in turn.
1551	Ottomans occupy Libya.
1711–1835	The Karamanli dynasty entails a series of local

	rulers for Tripoli, although the Ottoman sultan is technically still in charge.	**April 1986**	The USA bombs Tripoli and Benghazi, killing Colonel Qaddafi's child.
19th century	The indigenous Sanusi movement rises in Cyrenaica and sparks a resistance against occupation.	**1991**	Two Libyan men are charged with bombing a US plane over the Scottish town of Lockerbie in 1988.
1912	Libya is colonised by Italy. Their occupation lasts 30 years.	**15 April 1992**	UN sanctions are imposed on Libya.
24 December 1951	Following World War II and an interim period of British and French administration, independence is finally declared. The United Kingdom of Libya, ruled by the Sanusi King Idris, is left with a legacy of poverty.	**1999**	UN sanctions are lifted. The UN finally accepts Libya's repeated offer to send the Lockerbie suspects to The Hague for trial. In July the Italian government apologises to Libya for the occupation.
1959	First oilfield discovered.	**2001**	The Constitutive Act of African Union, set in motion by Colonel Qaddafi's desire for a 'United States of Africa', is signed by 41 countries.
1 September 1969	A military coup leads to a new leader: Colonel Muammar Qaddafi.	**19 December 2003**	Colonel Qaddafi renounces the country's nuclear, chemical and biological weapons programmes.
1970s and 1980s	During a period of extreme and contradictory home politics, Libya is implicated in various international terrorist attacks, and simultaneously at war with neighbouring Chad. Libya becomes increasingly isolated.	**2006**	Libya is taken off the US government list of states sponsoring terrorism.
		2008	Italy pledges compensation to Libya for the occupation.

Politics

Libyan politics have long been dominated by Colonel Muammar Qaddafi, who is now the longest-ruling country leader in the world. Despite this consistency, things have been far from quiet on the Libyan political scene in the past. With its international relations growing increasingly positive and open, Libya finally seems to be enjoying a period of political stability. However, there is still a general reluctance to discuss politics in public and visitors should be sensitive to this during conversations with Libyans.

Since the revolution

Qaddafi's government has always been radical and controversial, with constant reinventions of policies and image. Following the revolution, a programme of extensive government control, including mass nationalisation, was instigated. All opposition was prevented but, for most Libyans, standards of living improved as social and economic development was prioritised. From the late 1970s to the late 1980s, the political climate darkened considerably. In 1977, Qaddafi renamed the country the Great Socialist People's Libyan Arab Jamahiriya (roughly 'Rule of the Masses'). He indicated that all Libyans would be considered participants in the governance of their country. The reality was less idealistic: 'revolutionary committees' persecuted anyone they judged to be less than wholly dedicated to the revolution. Qaddafi later criticised their methods, but much damage had been done. Libyans were also suffering financially as a result of a failing economy, worsened by the years of sanctions.

International relations

In international relations, as in the economy, Libya's journey has been a dramatic and complicated one. The mending of relations has been an ongoing process since UN sanctions were lifted in 1999. Towards the end of the sanctions, other African nations had begun to show solidarity with Libya. South African President Nelson Mandela famously visited the country in 1997. Despite doubts around the verdict in the case, the Libyan government has now paid substantial compensation to the families of the Lockerbie victims. Libya has been accused of supporting certain terrorist acts, yet Colonel Qaddafi has publicly criticised Islamic fundamentalism. His 2003 renouncement of Libya's nuclear, chemical and biological weapons programmes was another major bridge-building act.

Colonel Qaddafi has long sought unity with other countries. Following an unsuccessful attempt with the Arab states, he pursued the African connection instead. This achieved far greater success: the Constitutive Act of African Union was signed by 41 states and ratified by 13 in 2001.

The future

A big question mark hangs over the future of Libyan politics. Colonel Qaddafi's son Seif al-Islam al-Qaddafi is a prominent figure in politics and the media, but he has denied that he will take over the leadership when his father dies. In recent years there has been marked progress in the country's economic status and standards of living. The financial difficulties of the past are slowly being repaired through reforms, but there is still a way to go. Half the Libyan workforce is currently employed by the government, unemployment is high and the oil industry dominates. In 2008, Colonel Qaddafi made another radical announcement: an intention to hand out oil revenue directly to Libyan citizens. Under this new scheme, if it goes ahead, responsibility for some public services will shift from the General People's Committees (or cabinet) to individual citizens.

Politics

Qaddafi wall-sized poster in the Jamahiriya Museum

Culture

Libyan culture reflects an intriguing balance of modernity and tradition, with the family and home at its heart. As socialising revolves around family occasions, Libya does not have strong customs of public entertainment or performance. There are artistic traditions, however, particularly in literature, music and dance. In addition, Libya has a rich and varied architectural heritage.

Architecture

Libya was left with an outstanding architectural legacy by the ancient colonisers from Greece, Rome and Byzantium. There are also many wonderful examples of Islamic, Berber and desert architecture.

Art and craft

Libyan art does not have a strong international profile. There are some modern painters who are fairly well known within Libya and who work with a range of mediums and styles. The website *www.libyanet.com* lists some prominent Libyan artists, along with their contact details and samples of their work. There are few designated art galleries in the country, but crafts are popular and a number of artisans open their studios to the public.

Literature

Libya has a great literary heritage, but few works have been translated into other languages. Prior to the revolution, writers were predominantly concerned with the pressing and oppressing issues of the times. After the revolution, the government elevated literature to a position of high public standing and publishing houses were established. One of the most famous modern writers is Tuareg writer Ibrahim al-Koni. Several of his desert-themed novels (*see 'Suggested reading and media', p153*) are available in English translation. Hisham Matar, an expatriate Libyan, won international acclaim for his poignant novel *In the Country of Men*, about 1970s Libya.

Music and dance

Music and dance are important elements of any Libyan celebration or festival. Folkloric Tuareg and Berber dances are performed, accompanied by traditional music, at local events around the country. At weddings, special types of lyrical music, called *mriskaawi* and *malouf*, are played. Although there are some popular

Camel riders at the Ghat festival

Libyan singers, most of the modern music played in the country is actually from elsewhere in North Africa or the Arab world.

Society and religion

'You cannot clap if you are single-handed' (translation of a Libyan proverb on the importance of joining together).

Although Libyans tend to have a strong sense of national and religious identity, family identity is even stronger. Libya's population of about 6.2 million equates to one of the lowest population densities in the world. The vast majority of Libyans (estimated 97 per cent) are of Arab or Berber descent and most are Sunni Muslims. Religion, practised with a characteristic lack of ostentation, has significant cultural influence. Minority cultural-linguistic groups include those Berbers who have retained their traditional languages, and the Tuareg (*see pp16–17*). Libya has small native Black African communities, concentrated in the oasis towns, as well as growing numbers of migrants from sub-Saharan Africa. There used to be a significant Jewish population until World War II and the creation of the State of Israel. There is a small population of Christians.

In the eyes of Libyan law, men and women are equal. Divorce is legal and forced marriage is illegal. In principle, women can do the same jobs as men for the same pay. These and other policies make Libya one of the most equal societies in the Arab world. However, traditional gender roles persist and men are dominant in the public sphere. Women are expected to dress modestly and the majority wear a headscarf, although this is not compulsory. In the south, arranged marriages between extended family members are still common, while in the north many young people meet their future spouses at school or university.

Tuareg culture

The Sahara and its people have fascinated visitors for centuries. In southern Libya, traditions and customs are very different from those in the north. Among the people who call the desert home are the traditionally nomadic Tuareg, or Kel Tamasheq, people. They share a common language and culture across country borders in Libya, Algeria, Niger, Sudan, Mali, Mauritania and Burkina Faso. They identify with several names, of which 'Tuareg' (a name originally coined by outsiders) is the most recently accepted. They are sometimes romantically described as 'the blue people of the Sahara'

The nomadic Tuareg call the Sahara home

because of their distinctive blue turbans (*taguelmoust*) and clothes. The turbans, in addition to providing effective protection from the harsh desert winds, are a symbolic garment. Unusually, in Tuareg culture it is men, rather than women, who are governed by social rules concerning the veiling of their faces. Traditionally, Tuareg men cover the lower part of their faces when in company, especially if there are men of higher community status present.

The Tuareg language, Tamasheq, has been observed to share features with the Berber language Tamazight, and it is generally thought that the Tuareg were originally Berbers. Nobody knows for certain where the Tuareg originated, but they are known to have lived in the Sahara since at least the time of the Arab invasion. As well as being informed by Islam, their culture is influenced by a rich tradition of mythology and folklore. There are echoes of ancient Egypt in their folklore and in the Tamasheq language.

The Tuareg people of southwest Libya know the landscape inside out and have many intriguing legends attached to certain places. One such place is Kaf Ajnoun (*see p115*), a

A Tuareg man

mountainous rock formation between the Jebel Acacus and the Algerian border. Kaf Ajnoun means 'Mountain of Ghosts' and was also known as 'Devil's Hill'. The Tuareg believed that *djinns* (genies) held council there. In the 19th century, at the height of European exploration of the Sahara, several explorers were tempted to climb Kaf Ajnoun, with varying levels of success.

Although the first appearances of Europeans in the deepest Sahara must have taken the locals by surprise, they were already used to strangers passing through. When trans-Saharan caravan trade was thriving, the Tuareg found various ways to make an independent living from the passing traders, for example by acting as paid protectors for the caravans. Many

Tuareg have renounced the nomadic way of life and moved to settled communities, but a fairly small number of families continues to live a traditional lifestyle in the desert of southwestern Libya.

Travellers on desert trips are likely to come across Tuareg traders selling their crafts. Many of the pieces are distinctive and culturally symbolic, especially the iconic 'Tuareg cross' or *croix d'Agadez* (named after a town in Niger). There are many variations in the design of the cross, but it always has the same significance. It is seen as an amulet imbued with the power to protect the wearer, to ward off the evil eye and, in some cases, to boost fertility. You may also come across jewellery inscribed with the symbols of the Tuareg alphabet.

Festivals and events

Festivals and events in Libya can be broadly grouped into three categories: religious celebrations, national holidays and local festivals. Most of the events listed below are traditional local festivals which have become significant dates in the cultural calendar. They are held annually unless otherwise stated. Islamic events take place on different dates each year. The main celebrations are for Eid al-Fitr at the end of Ramadan, Eid al-Adha, and Moulid an-Nabi, celebrating the Prophet Mohammed's birthday.

Key dates for the next few years in the Islamic calendar are provided in the feature 'Islamic Libya' (*see p33*). Dates for public holidays in Libya are listed in the 'Directory' section (*see p153*).

Spring festivals (late February to April)

Houn

This remote desert town is the location of an annual sweet-making competition and festival celebrating the coming of spring. The goal is to make the most extravagant sweets possible.

Germa

The desert town of Germa hosts a community-centred spring festival of traditional dance. This festival is not held every year.

Nalut

The town of Nalut, high in the mountains of the Jebel Nafusa region, also hosts a spring festival in April with traditional dance, music and parades.

Qasr festival, Kabaw

This festival is a celebration of the area's Berber traditions and folklore, and first took place in 1990 after the *qasr* (granary or 'castle') was restored. It is not held every year at present.

August

Awussu festival, Zuara

In the heat of summer, the residents of this coastal town in eastern Tripolitania take to the beach for a festival of sailing, swimming and dancing.

September

Revolution Day

Of the various national holidays in the Libyan calendar, all of which are marked with public speeches, 1 September is the most significant by far. There is a military parade, plus speeches and rallies across the country.

CELEBRATIONS

Celebrations in Libya tend to be family affairs, although the wider community is often included as well. Weddings are the most extravagant manifestation of the Libyan love of celebration, while on the other end of the scale Fridays provide the most frequent excuse. Marriage ceremonies are generally held on a Thursday, with festivities lasting usually three to four days and sometimes even stretching over a whole week. Huge numbers of guests are invited for banquets and traditional dancing. On typical Fridays, families flock to the beaches or parks for picnics. Religious events are celebrated with special feasts and public festivities, generally involving music and fireworks.

October or November
Ghadames

The festival held annually in Ghadames is one of Libya's biggest local events. It takes place over three days (the month depends on when Ramadan falls), during which the main action moves from the new town to the old city and then out into the desert. Traditional dances are performed all over town throughout the festival. The old city provides a unique setting for this cultural celebration. A number of the old houses are opened to serve as the venues for re-enactments of old-style ceremonies.

Late December
Acacus festival, Ghat

The Acacus festival takes place in Ghat around New Year. A celebration of Tuareg culture, it includes traditional dancing and musical performances.

A female singing group in traditional dress at the Ghat festival

Highlights

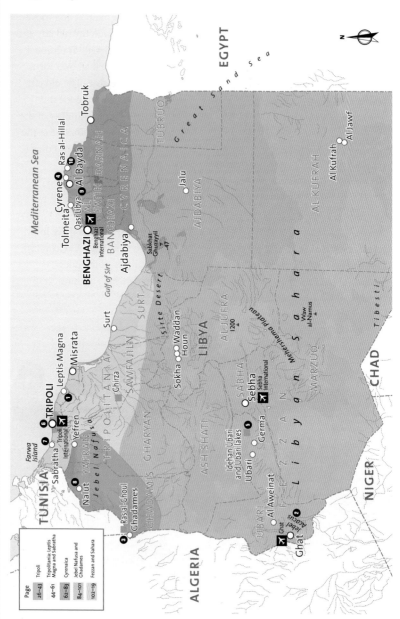

❶ Leptis Magna Take an evocative journey back in time, discovering fascinating monument after fascinating monument, at the best-preserved Roman city in Africa (*see pp48–55*).

❷ Jebel Acacus Marvel at the wealth of prehistoric rock paintings and engravings tucked away in one of the Sahara's most dramatic landscapes (*see pp103–9*).

❸ Ghadames Wander the labyrinthine covered streets of this beautiful old caravan city. Visit a traditional house and learn about the unique culture that thrived here for centuries (*see pp86–91*).

❹ Cyrene Visit the extensive ruins of the most significant ancient Greek city in Libya, a scenic site with monuments bearing witness to the region's long and varied history (*see pp65–9*).

❺ Idehan Ubari and Ubari lakes Leave civilisation behind for a stunning Saharan landscape of sweeping golden dunes and palm-fringed oasis lakes (*see p110*).

❻ Tripoli's medina Take in the capital's atmospheric old town, where the colourful shops, attractive architecture and the friendliness of the people all add to the charm (*see pp27–31*).

❼ Sabratha Visit an ancient Roman city with distinctive character, home to one of the most impressive theatres of antiquity and a collection of stunning mosaics (*see pp56–60*).

❽ Nalut Explore a fantastical 'castle', or fortified granary, a spectacular example of Berber architecture in the country (*see p93*).

❾ Qasr Libya View some of the most significant examples of Libya's mosaic-rich heritage: a set of Byzantine panels depicting a fascinating range of scenes (*see p78*).

❿ Ras al-Hillal Enjoy stunning coastal scenery and explore the ruins of Byzantine churches at this picturesque spot in Libya's greenest corner (*see pp82–3*).

The marketplace at Leptis Magna

Suggested itineraries

Long weekend

Tripoli has fantastic city-break potential, especially when combined with a visit to nearby historical or cultural attractions. The splendid ancient sites of Leptis Magna and Sabratha are both within easy day-trip distance. The Berber *qasrs* of the Jebel Nafusa are a little further afield, but still reachable in a long weekend.

Coastal Tripolitania

Spend your first full day in Tripoli. A morning visit to the excellent Jamahiriya Museum (*see p37*) followed by an afternoon exploring the medina (*see pp27–31 & 34–5*) will show the city at its best. Add lunch in a medina restaurant, tea in a traditional tea house and an evening stroll to the Jamal Abdel Nasser mosque (*see p42*). Visit Sabratha on the second day. After spending several hours at the site, there should still be time for a dip in the Mediterranean or some more shopping in Tripoli. Leptis Magna is best saved until last and allocated a full day, as there is so much to see at Libya's most famous site.

Tripoli and the Jebel Nafusa

Spend a day exploring Tripoli (*see above*), before heading into the Jebel Nafusa. Visit the incredible Berber *qasrs* (granaries or 'castles') at Qasr al-Haj, Kabaw and Nalut, each of which is unique. Spend the night in Nalut, then head back east towards the town of Gharyan the next day. Make a slight detour to take in the view from the hilltop village of Tarmeisa. In Gharyan you can peruse a vast roadside pottery market (*see pp98–9*) before visiting one of the underground 'troglodyte' houses. Return to Tripoli in time for a leisurely evening meal.

An alternative itinerary is to set off as early as possible for the Jebel Nafusa, see the area in one day and skip the night in Nalut in favour of a night in Gharyan. If you travel as part of a group, it may be possible to stay a night in a troglodyte house, including a traditional meal. You could then fit in the pottery market the next morning before returning to Tripoli for some last-minute shopping.

One week

A week is long enough to make an excursion into the Sahara. Alternatively, you could visit Ghadames or embark on a cultural odyssey of the ancient cities along the coast.

Southwestern Libya

Fly from Tripoli to Sebha then head southwest into the Sahara on the road to Ubari. Distances between the amazing sights in this region are vast, so this itinerary involves a lot of driving. Travel to the Jebel Acacus via the historical town of Germa, the rock art of Wadi Methkandoush and the massive dunes of Idehan Murzuq. Stay two full days in the Acacus, before winding a slow route back up to the main road and heading east to the Ubari region. Allow a full day to see the beautiful Ubari lakes, saving some of the most iconic desert scenery for last. A more detailed route including these sights is provided in the 'Desert experience' tour (*see pp116–17*).

Tripolitania and Ghadames

Spend your first morning visiting Sabratha. A picnic lunch is a good idea, before driving into the Jebel Nafusa to Qasr al-Haj and Nalut. Spend a night in Nalut, before continuing to Ghadames. Arriving in time for lunch, you should be able to eat in a traditional house in the old city. Have a restful afternoon before rounding off the day with a trip to the fortress at

The Berber *qasr* at Nalut

A sea of sand dunes at the Ubari lakes

Ras al-Ghoul, followed by climbing
the nearby dunes to watch the sunset.
The next morning, visit the museum
before exploring the old city. This easily
merits a whole day's leisurely
exploration, but it can be fitted into a
morning to leave time for an afternoon
camel ride. On day four, drive back
through the Jebel Nafusa to Gharyan,
where you can unwind with an
atmospheric stay in a troglodyte house.
Return to Tripoli on day five and spend
some time in the city before setting
off the next day on an excursion to
Leptis Magna.

Cities of Cyrenaica

After spending your first day in Tripoli,
take a morning flight to Benghazi for
some more city sightseeing. Aim to fit
in Souq al-Jreed (*see p64*), the Acacus
House and a meal at one of Benghazi's
interesting restaurants. On day three,
drive along the coast into northern
Cyrenaica. Stop off briefly to see the
Turkish fort at Tocra, before continuing
to Tolmeita and then on to Apollonia to
spend the night. On day four, take a
morning excursion to the hilly villages
of Ras al-Hillal and L'Atrun for
spectacular views and Byzantine

churches, before an afternoon visit to the site at Apollonia. Dedicate the whole of the following day to Cyrene, the highlight of the region. Drive back to Benghazi on day six, via the mosaic museum at Qasr Libya. Depending on flight times, you may then need to spend another night in Benghazi before flying back to Tripoli.

Two weeks or longer

Having two weeks or more to spend in Libya will give you a chance to see many sights which are far away from each other.

Highlights of the north

Spend the first week following the 'Cities of Cyrenaica' itinerary (*see above*). Relax in Tripoli for a day, before heading into the Jebel Nafusa and on to Ghadames. Visit the Berber *qasr* towns on the way there and Gharyan on the way back. After two days in Ghadames and two days of travelling, you will still have time to spend a day each at Sabratha and Leptis Magna, with Tripoli as your base.

Highlights of the desert

Start by driving from Tripoli to Ghadames through the Jebel Nafusa, stopping off at Qasr al-Haj, Kabaw and Nalut. After a couple of days in Ghadames, strike out southbound across the desert on an epic journey to Ghat. This roughly 600km (370-mile) trip crosses the vast Hamada al-Hamra ('Red Plain') and just touches on the

Ubari sand-sea. You will have to camp two nights in the desert en route. Visit the old city of Ghat (*see p111*), before immersing yourself in the Jebel Acacus. Loop round to the Ubari lakes via Wan Caza, Wadi Methkandoush and Germa (*see pp112–14*). If you have time, you could embark on another very long drive back to Tripoli. Go north via Sebha and the oasis towns of Waddan and Houn (*see p115*). Hitting the coast at the town of Misrata, head west and stop off at Leptis Magna before returning to Tripoli. If time does not allow, or if you are not so keen on long desert drives, take a flight from Sebha instead.

A shady street in Tripoli

Tripoli

Libya's capital city is also one of its most enchanting destinations. With its animated medina (old town), remarkable buildings and palm-lined coastal promenade, Tripoli merits leisurely exploration. Woven into the fabric of the city is the welcoming, laidback attitude of its people, providing a positive introduction to the country. Consistently inhabited since Phoenician times, Tripoli has a long history of change, turmoil and development, out of which a fascinating modern city has risen.

In Roman times, the city where Tripoli now stands was called Oea. Together the cities of Oea, Leptis Magna and Sabratha made up Tripolitania ('Land of Three Cities'), also known as the 'tripolis'. The Roman era was one of the city's heydays, but this was brought to an abrupt end by the destructive occupation of the Vandals. Tripoli would not thrive again until the Arabic invasion, when it was given a new name, Tarablus (which remains the

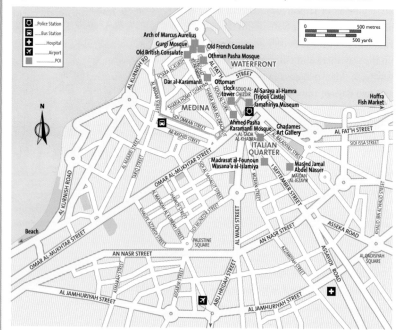

The lights of Tripoli's promenade

Arabic name today), and a new lease of life. The winds of change continued to blow through the city, with subsequent occupations by the Spanish, the Maltese Knights of St John, the Ottoman Turks and the Italians. Despite the feuding and social implications of the occupations, Tripoli prospered. The majority of the buildings in the medina date from the Ottoman era, while many of those outside the old city walls were constructed by the Italians. The only remnant of old Oea is the Arch of Marcus Aurelius, although the Arabs also used some of the original Roman foundations when rebuilding the ruined city.

Following the devastation of World War II, the discovery of oil turned Tripoli's fortunes around again. More recently, Libya's improved relations with the outside world have allowed its capital to open up and become increasingly cosmopolitan, while retaining the traditional culture and rich fabric of history that make it distinctive.

MEDINA

A labyrinth of lanes and passages, many shaded by stone arches, climbing plants or wooden slats, make up Tripoli's charming medina. Entering this ancient walled section of the city brings Tripoli's history to life. Until the 19th century, the city was contained within the medina walls, which brushed right along the seafront. The oldest section of the wall dates from the 4th century, but most of the buildings standing today were built in the Turkish period. Whitewashed earth and limestone is the

Old colonial architecture in Tripoli's medina

the medina is a bustling, functional part of the city. Approximately 3,500 people live within the walls, while the markets, shops, hotels, restaurants and public buildings provide work for 65,000, and the mosques are still very much in use. Unlike elsewhere in Tripoli, in the medina most streets have signs in Roman lettering.

Arch of Marcus Aurelius

Standing at the northern corner of the medina, the grand Arch of Marcus Aurelius, built in the 2nd century, is all that remains of the ancient city of Oea. The story goes that the arch was protected by a prophecy that people would be cursed if they removed a single one of its stones. It was built as a triumphal arch, a sign of wealth and significance, at the harbour entrance to the city. The figures carved into the stone include the god Apollo and goddess Minerva, who were revered as mythical guardians of Oea. Today, the arch can be admired from various angles, including from the Athar Restaurant balconies. It is particularly worth seeing at night, lit in a golden hue.

Mosques

There are 38 mosques in the medina and they are some of the old city's finest, best-preserved buildings. They were mainly constructed over the centuries of Ottoman rule and were named after their founders or important figures of the time. Many of these individuals are buried in the

foundation of the architecture, with carved wood, marble and ceramic details adding elegance, finesse and colour.

Sadly, many of the whitewashed buildings now have an aged, crumbling look. The medina was also greatly damaged during the Italian occupation and World War II. Some skilful renovations have been carried out in recent years, as evidenced in a handful of buildings open to the public. These include the Zumit Hotel (*see pp161–2*) and Karamanli House (*see p30*). Far from being a vast museum, however, tombs of their namesake mosques. The biggest mosque is the Ahmed Pasha Karamanli Mosque, while one of the oldest is the Othman Pasha Mosque and Madrasa, which still has a functioning school.

The **Gurgi Mosque**, located near the Arch, definitely merits a visit. In keeping with the typical style, the exterior is un-showy and blends with neighbouring buildings, while the interior is exquisite. The prayer hall includes an architecturally eye-catching domed ceiling and marble pillars. There is also beauty in the details, such as the intricately patterned mosaic

VISITING MOSQUES

Many mosques in Libya welcome non-Muslim visitors, although some do not. They do not typically have set opening hours, so unless you are on a guided tour, you may need to knock for the caretaker or ask around in the vicinity. Avoid visiting on Fridays around noon. Both men and women should wear clothing that covers their legs and shoulders and women should not wear anything tight-fitting or revealing. Shoes must be removed before entering the prayer hall. Women are generally not required to wear headscarves, but it is considered respectful.

of ceramic tiles which forms the floor, and the delicate stonework in the niches and domes.

The Arch of Marcus Aurelius is the northern entrance to the medina

Public buildings and houses

The medina has a number of magnificent buildings which were once colonial offices or private homes for the rich, or both at different points in their history. It was typical for medina buildings to be designed around open courtyards to allow residents or users to enjoy private outdoor spaces. Many of the houses had two levels, with balconies and arched doorways leading to the indoor rooms. The following are examples of traditional buildings which are open to the public.

Dar al-Karamanli (Karamanli House)

The Karamanli House was built in the early 19th century as a residence for Yusuf Karamanli, one of the rulers of the Karamanli dynasty, and his harem.

Artisan pieces in the Copper Souk

Having housed such a prolific inhabitant, it is an example of truly luxurious accommodation. There is a fountain in the centre of the internal courtyard and many rooms branching off around it. The building now functions as a museum, with reconstructions of traditional rooms and exhibits of items from clothing to weapons. It is located to the south of the landmark Roman pillar crossroads. *Sharia Homet Gharyan. Open: Sat–Thur 9am–5pm. Admission & camera/video charges.*

Old British Consulate

This elegant building, which now epitomises peace and serenity in the middle of the busy medina, has a controversial history. Although it was originally built in 1744 as a residence (for Ahmed Pasha, founder of the Karamanli dynasty), it was soon transformed into the British Consulate office and used as a starting point for colonial expeditions into Africa. Its functions now, as a scientific library and example of architectural heritage, are much less inflammatory. *Sharia Hara Kbira. Open: Sat–Thur 9am–5pm. Admission & camera/video charges.*

Old French Consulate

The Old French Consulate, which dates back to 1630, making it a century older than the British version, is also used as a library and a museum of sorts. There are restored offices on the first floor

A display of spices at the souk

and a small art exhibition space. The roof space has good views over the medina, but whether you will be able to access this depends on the availability of the caretaker and the key.
Zenghat el-Fransis. Open: Sat–Thur 9am–5pm. Admission & camera/video charges.

Souks

The souks of the medina are a fascinating place to shop and there is a bewildering array of items on offer. Even just wandering through the twisting market streets and seeing how the character of the shops changes around every corner is an interesting pastime. The main shopping district stretches to the left of **Souq al-Muscir**, which is the street leading from the Al-Sada al-Khadra (Green Square) entrance, and around **Souq al-Turk**.

This main street is made colourful by the rugs displayed outside the shops, striking a contrast with the white-washed walls and arches overhead.

Additional small shops can be found throughout the medina, generally advertised by the items spilling out into the streets. These wares, such as patterned rugs and copper lanterns, brighten the walkways and add considerably to the atmosphere of the medina. One of the most striking areas is **Souq al-Ghizdir (Copper Souk)**, a narrow lane located behind the Ottoman clock tower. The shops here double as open workshops for the copper artisans, and visitors can watch as they create minarets, lanterns and other pieces. This is a vivid place of sights and sounds likely to make you feel like you have stepped back centuries, or strayed into Aladdin's cave.

Islamic Libya

Libya has been an Islamic country since the 7th century, having been conquered by Arab tribes just two decades after the beginning of the Islamic calendar in AD 622. Religion forms an important part of the culture and, although Libyans are not ostentatious about their beliefs, the tenets of Islamic faith are almost universally observed. Understanding these will help you gain some insight into the traditions of the country. The Islamic religion has five pillars: profession of faith (*shahada*) to Allah and Mohammed as his prophet, prayer (*sala*), alms-giving (*zakat*), fasting (*sawm*) and pilgrimage (*haj*).

Prayers are said five times a day, whether in the mosque, which is most important on Fridays at noon, or elsewhere. As Muslims must pray facing the direction of Mecca, mosques feature a *mihrab*, a niche in the wall that signposts the right way to face. Each mosque has an *imam*, the important religious figure of Islam, who leads the Friday noon prayers from a *minbar*, a pulpit next to the *mihrab*. Both the *minbar* and *mihrab* are often grand in design. The structure of the prayer hall is typically simple, consisting of an open-plan room with columns separating a series of aisles. However, the floors, ceilings and columns are often decorated with elaborately beautiful patterns. Between the outer walls of the mosque and the prayer hall is a *sahn* (enclosed courtyard) and there are generally also other auxiliary rooms within the compound. The mosques were originally linked to hammams (Turkish baths) and *madrasas* (Quranic schools), some of which remain in use today. The prayer hall is also a serene place for individual prayer at other times. Essentially, the mosque functions as a centre for the community.

In fulfilment of the fasting aspect of the five pillars of Islam, during Ramadan, the ninth month of the Islamic calendar, Muslims should fast from sunrise until sunset every day and should not let anything, cigarettes included, pass their lips. The tenet of alms-giving requires Muslims to donate part of their income to the poor. And the commitment to pilgrimage relates to the famous journey to Mecca. Every Muslim who is able to go is expected to travel there at least once in their life in order to be spiritually cleansed of all past sins. When they return, the

Elaborate decoration inside Gurgi Mosque

pilgrims are seen as deserving of increased respect from the community and can advertise their *haji* status. Other people may call them *haj* or *haji* and they might decorate the front door of their house as a symbol. In the old city of Ghadames, people did this in a distinctive way: they affixed rows of small leather studs in red, yellow and green to the doors.

IMPORTANT DATES IN THE ISLAMIC CALENDAR

	2009	2010	2011	2012	2013
Ramadan starts	21 Aug	11 Aug	1 Aug	20 Jul	9 Jul
Eid al-Fitr (end of Ramadan)	20 Sept	9 Sept	30 Aug	19 Aug	8 Aug
Eid al-Adha	27 Nov	16 Nov	6 Nov	26 Oct	15 Oct
Al-Hijra (Islamic New Year)	18 Dec	7 Dec	26 Nov	15 Nov	4 Nov

Walk: Tripoli medina

This walk is a good introduction to Tripoli's old city. There is an emphasis on architecture, with several restored buildings from the Ottoman era featuring on the route, alongside the remaining traces of Tripoli's Roman past. The route also passes some of the medina's most vibrant shopping streets, or souks.

This winding route covers about 2km (1¼ miles). Allow two hours to stop off at all the sights, longer if you want to shop.

Start outside the castle or museum. Walk away from the seafront, then turn right up Souq al-Muscir.

1 Ottoman clock tower

This 19th-century building is one of the medina's most distinctive landmarks.
Walk left behind the clock tower into Souq al-Ghizdir, the copper souk.

2 Souq al-Ghizdir (Copper Souk)

Wander down this most evocative of lanes, peeping into the workshops.
At the end, turn left on Souq Ettbbakha, then right onto 'Suk Etturk' (or Souq al-Turk, see p31). Take a left (Sc Arba Arsat) and walk to the end.

3 Al Arba'a Arsaht (Roman column crossroads)

The crossroads is distinctive with Roman columns at each corner.
Turn right here. After a short distance there is another (single) Roman pillar in front of a small square.

4 Buildings near Roman pillar

Opposite the pillar on the left is the restored Banco di Roma. Next door is the former Catholic cathedral. The Turkish prison is on the other side of the square.
Take the narrow street on the top left of the square (Zenghat el-Fransis). The street passes the Old French Consulate before opening onto a view of the arch.

5 Arch of Marcus Aurelius

The small square is dominated by the arch, one of the most iconic landmarks of Tripoli (*see p28*). Just to your left is the restored Zumit Hotel (*see pp161–2*).
The minaret of the Gurgi Mosque is visible behind the arch.

6 Gurgi Mosque

Avoid arriving at Friday prayer time and you should be able to look around the beautiful interior (*see p29*).
Take Sciara al-Kuash and walk a little way along.

7 Old British Consulate

This is a restored medina building that is open to visitors (*see p30*).

Retrace your steps back to the Roman column crossroads. Just south of here is the Karamanli House.

8 Dar al-Karamanli

Go inside for a glimpse of this extravagant 19th-century townhouse (*see p30*).

Continue straight on along Sharia Jama ad-Draghut. At the series of white arches, turn left onto Zenghat Inse. Follow the

road to the right, turn left (signed Suk el Liffa) and then right (Suk Essiagha). On the right is a covered souq.

9 Souq al-Rabaa

This is a particularly labyrinthine section of the medina. Next to the souq is a courtyard which once served as a stopping point for caravans.

Past the square, turn left and you will find yourself in a muddled, improvised souk. Walk straight through back onto the main Souq al-Muscir. Go right to exit the medina.

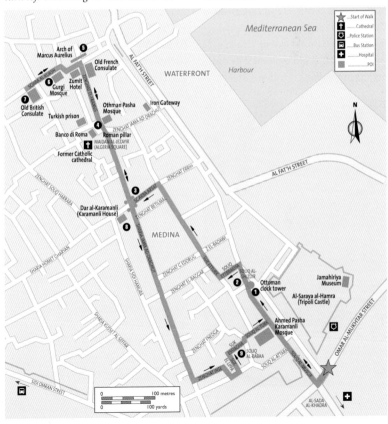

AL-SADA AL-KHADRA (GREEN SQUARE) AREA

Also known as Martyrs' Square, Green Square, just outside the medina, has a pleasant, almost festive atmosphere if you can overlook the traffic that speeds around the perimeter. In the years following the revolution, the newly purpose-built square was used for public rallies of support for Colonel Qaddafi. Nowadays, it is still the centre of public events, hosting everything from speeches to fairgrounds. A curious combination of floodlights, fairy lights, horse-drawn carriages and cars gives the square a unique character. And facing the square are two of Tripoli's most fascinating old buildings: its castle and its museum.

A courtyard at Al-Saraya al-Hamra

PASHAS, PLOTS AND PIRATES

Throughout the Ottoman era, power struggles, lawlessness and leadership plots were the order of the day in Tripoli. Pirates had roamed the coast unchallenged for years. At one point the notorious pirate king Khair ad-Din, known as Barbarossa or Redbeard, effectively had control. The Ottoman sultan delegated authority over the city to a pasha (governor), ignoring the pirates of the seas as well as the murderous goings-on in the seat of power, Tripoli Castle. The pashas did not fare well: most were assassinated or deposed by rivals. In 1790, Yusuf Karamanli, heir of the ruling dynasty, actually shot his own brothers in order to secure his succession.

Al-Saraya al-Hamra (Tripoli Castle)

The castle is one of Tripoli's main landmarks. Until the 1970s, when the main road along the seafront was built on reclaimed land, the sea flowed right up to the walls of the medina and the castle directly overlooked the water. It is an imposing fortress of a building, thought to date from the Arab invasion in the 7th century AD, although many of the interior features were designed during much later periods. Unfortunately, the castle was closed at the time of writing and there were no immediate plans to reopen it. Permission to look around can be sought from the Department of Antiquities through your tour company, although there are no guarantees. Inside, there is a distinctive atmosphere, created by an air of abandonment and a maze-like layout of

The fountain in the centre of Green Square

courtyards. The courtyards are separated by arches and steps, and ornamented by decorative tiles, old-fashioned lamps and overgrown plants. Note the huge strangler fig tree, planted by the Italians, which completely fills one of the courtyards.

Jamahiriya Museum

Tripoli's Jamahiriya Museum is a wonderful introduction to Libya's extensive history, from the time of Saharan rock art through the classical period to the revolution and present day. The museum has five levels. The ground floor is by far the most fascinating and you will probably want to concentrate your time here. Most of the signs are written only in Arabic, although there are general overviews of the rooms in English. Guides are compulsory and bags have to be left in a (free) cloakroom

by the small shop. Overviews of each floor are given below with details of the most interesting rooms.

Open: Tue–Sun 9am–1pm & 2–5pm.
Admission & camera charges.

Ground floor (galleries 1–9)
Gallery 1 is also the entrance hall and serves as an intriguing visual introduction to what you will see in the rest of the museum. The eclectic mix of exhibits includes a lovely Roman statue of Venus, which was retrieved from Europe relatively recently, and a VW Beetle, the car used by the young Colonel Qaddafi during the revolution. There is also a mural of Tripoli in the 17th century, a mosaic from Leptis Magna and an approximately 2,000-year-old stone tomb representing pre-Islamic Libyan culture. One particular highlight is a large wall map of the

A marble statue of the Three Graces at Jamahiriya Museum

country with differently coloured lights activated by pressing buttons. The lights show the concentration of sights from the prehistoric, Punic and Greek, Roman and Islamic periods, as well as the old Saharan trade routes and the location of Libya's museums.

Galleries 2–4 cover the prehistoric era. These rooms showcase the ancient crafts of the Libyan Sahara, from ceramics to rock paintings and carvings. The rock art here has been stunningly reproduced from the originals deep in the desert on cave walls. Look out for the wedding party scene showing women doing each other's hair, one of the clearest and most unusual depictions of ancient society.

Gallery 5 is dedicated to Libyan heritage from the classical period, but distinct from the Punic, Greek and Roman civilisations. It focuses particularly on the Garamantes Empire and includes stone carvings of people, animals and scenes from everyday life.

Gallery 6 is Phoenician or Punic. Compared with the rich archaeological reminders of the Greek and Roman civilisations in Libya, little remains from the Phoenician (Punic) settlements. The few artefacts in this gallery include stone plaques with Punic writing and the symbol for the goddess Tanit.

Galleries 7 and 8 introduce the Greek influence in northeastern Libya. Highlights include a model of the impressive Temple of Zeus at Cyrene, as it was in the city's heyday, and an elegant statue of the Three Graces

from Cyrene. This statue dates from the 3rd century BC, but has been beautifully preserved.

Gallery 9 is the Roman area and houses an amazing collection from the ancient Roman sites of Tripolitania. This spacious gallery is split into three rooms, one for Leptis Magna, one for Sabratha and a central area between the two. The lovely mosaic which covers much of the floor in the central room is a rare remnant of the old city of Oea. Just inside the door in the Leptis Magna room is a beautiful, intricately rendered mosaic of birds and flowers. This was found in a villa near Leptis, but most of the artefacts in the room were taken from the site itself. They

A mosaic in the Sabratha room

A fishing scene in one of Jamahiriya's well-preserved mosaics

include a number of outstanding statues of gods and goddesses and a large 'Four Seasons' mosaic. In the middle of the room is a model of Leptis as it would have looked in its prime. The Sabratha room also contains a

PRACTICALITIES OF SITE VISITS

Most museums and sites charge a small entrance fee and there is often an additional token charge for taking photographs or using a video camera. Bags are not permitted at some of the sites, such as Leptis Magna and Tripoli's Jamahiriya Museum, and must be left in lockers or vehicles. Where this is the case, it should still be fine to carry a clear plastic bag with essential items. Also, visitors must be accompanied by a tour guide at many of the attractions. This can be the guide responsible for your whole stay in Libya or a site-specific guide.

model representation of the city. Sabratha is known for its mosaics and this gallery has some stunning examples, from the legend of Pegasus to everyday scenes such as fishing. The statues here include an angelic sleeping Cupid.

First floor (galleries 10–14)

Galleries 10 and 11 also contain some Roman artefacts, while galleries 12–14 show the Byzantine period. The balcony-style design of gallery 10 enables visitors to look down over gallery 9 while wandering around displays of small Roman items such as oil lamps, coins and pottery. Gallery 11 is an extension of the Leptis Magna room, devoted specifically to the Arch of Septimius Severus. The most interesting features of the Byzantine galleries are stone windows from old Byzantine churches.

Second floor (galleries 15–30)
The second floor contains a varied display of artefacts from all over the country. Some of the galleries are decidedly more interesting than others. Gallery 15 is dominated by an arch made of stone, brick and palm in the Islamic architectural style. Gallery 19 has a noteworthy model of the castle, a map of ancient Oea and reconstructions of rooms in the traditional styles of Ghadames and Tripolitania, among other exhibits. Gallery 20 and the linking corridor to Gallery 21 are worth a quick look for their cultural artefacts. There is a series of mannequins dressed up in diverse traditional costumes, some more reconstructed rooms and an eye-catching collection of objects including jewellery and swords.

Third floor (galleries 31–47)
The galleries on this floor are also of inconsistent merit. Gallery 31 is dedicated to the Libyan resistance during the years of Italian rule and features photographs of national hero Omar al-Mukhtar. In galleries 32–7, the theme progresses to the revolution years, with Colonel Qaddafi naturally taking centre stage. Finally there are the natural history galleries (38–47), which are a bit of a disappointment compared with most of the rest of the museum,

as many of the exhibits are either uninspiring or somewhat macabre.

ITALIAN QUARTER
To the east of Green Square stretches Tripoli's Italian quarter, another distinctive corner of the city. Much of the architecture here is in a colonial, Italianate style. It is a great district for wandering around, as well as for finding interesting information about Tripoli and Libya. Head to Fergiani's Bookshop (*see p144*) for general information, or to the **Libyan Studies Centre** (*Sharia Sidi al-Bahul. Tel: (021) 444 6988. Open: by appointment*) for more in-depth reading. The centre has a library (with books in English) and a collection of historical photographs. The **Ghadames Art Gallery** (*Sharia 1 September. Tel: (021) 333 6666. Open: Sat–Thur 10am–2pm & 5–9pm*) is a source of unusual souvenirs, with old photographs, paintings and drawings of Tripoli and elsewhere in Libya for sale.

**Madrasat al-Founoun Wasana'a al-Islamiya
(Islamic Arts and Crafts School)**
The school is housed in an elegant building set around two courtyards, an attractive location for the teaching of various traditional crafts. This is an interesting building to visit because of its singular design and history. Initially a school in the Ottoman era, it has now been restored to its original function after a spell as a prison during the Italian occupation.

Masjed Jamal Abdel Nasser Mosque, a converted cathedral

Sharia 1 September. Open: Sat–Thur 10am–6pm. Free admission.

Maidan al-Jezayir (Algeria Square)

The highlight of Algeria Square is the **Masjed Jamal Abdel Nasser**, a former Catholic cathedral which was converted into a mosque after the revolution. The architectural transformation of the building took over 30 years to complete and the result is strikingly graceful. Non-Muslims are not allowed to enter, but the exterior alone is definitely worth a look. It is particularly eye-catching at night when floodlit.

WATERFRONT AREA

A number of refreshment stalls and café tables have sprung up along Tripoli's promenade, giving it a laidback Mediterranean vibe. The only shame is that the seafront is separated from the rest of Tripoli by a hectic main road. Still, the waterfront is attractive, especially at night, when it is illuminated and bustling with people sitting in the parkland, fishing along the harbour and enjoying the tea gardens. The parkland, which shadows the promenade on the other side of the main road, is a splash of green breaking up the white of the city. Palm trees and flowering plants including bougainvillea, oleander and red hibiscus line the streets around the waterfront, adding to the leafy coastal feel. The majestic-looking building facing the harbour on the other side of the castle from Green Square is the National Bank.

Beach

The beach to the west of central Tripoli boasts a surprisingly clear sea, which is shallow for a considerable way from the shore. The beach is popular with local families and has a family-friendly atmosphere. A distinctive holiday vibe is in the air in the summer months as tables, chairs and beach umbrellas are laid out on the sand.

Fish Market

The fish market is located on the seafront 5.5km (3½ miles) east of the

SAFETY IN THE CITY

Tripoli is an incredibly safe city and the risk of crime is extremely low. There are some slightly less salubrious areas, notably the western entrances to the medina and the Sharia ar-Rashid district, southwest of the medina. Many locals would recommend avoiding walking through the medina at night as a precaution. The biggest potential threat by far is posed by the high volume and speed of cars. There are no pedestrian crossings and the local way of getting across several lanes of traffic is simply to step out at an opportune moment. The road circling Green Square, with its several lanes, is definitely one to watch. Always exercise caution and tackle roads one lane at a time.

harbour, along the road leading to Tajura and on to Leptis Magna. It is fairly small but packed with all sorts of fish and seafood. There are restaurants around the edge of the market, where you can ask for your choice of fresh fish to be cooked for you (*see pp164–6*).

The beach with the Tripoli skyline, including 'upturned bottle' buildings

Tripolitania: Leptis Magna and Sabratha

In addition to Tripoli itself, there are two very good reasons to visit the coastal Tripolitania region: the ancient cities of Leptis Magna and Sabratha, which made up two-thirds of the 'tripolis' and which stand today as stunning reminders of a grand Roman past. Leptis is the largest, best-preserved Roman city in Africa, while Sabratha boasts a beautiful setting, a stunning theatre and some lovely mosaics.

Italian archaeologists began excavations at Leptis and Sabratha in the early 20th century, uncovering incredible ruins which had lain buried under the sand for hundreds of years. Initially established as trading ports by the Phoenicians, or 'people of the sea', the cities had flourished under ancient Rome. The decline of the empire and a series of natural disasters, most notably a devastating earthquake in AD 365, took a heavy toll. Although

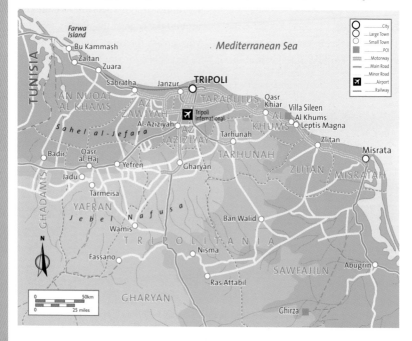

Mediterranean landscape near Leptis Magna

both cities survived into the Islamic era, they were eventually abandoned. Leptis and Sabratha have both been designated UNESCO World Heritage Sites since 1982.

The administrative region of Tripolitania stretches inland into the Jebel Nafusa and east to the border of Cyrenaica. However, the sights of interest are concentrated in a fairly small area. Both Leptis Magna and Sabratha are within easy day-trip distance of Tripoli. Leptis is 123km (76 miles) east of the capital and Sabratha is just 69km (43 miles) to the west. The sea views, which add to the considerable charm of the ruins, can also be enjoyed from various points along Tripolitania's coast. The white-sand beaches to the west of Sabratha are particularly attractive. Another highlight of the region is the mosaic-strewn Villa Sileen, near Leptis Magna. It was closed for renovations at the time of writing but is sure to be worth a visit when it reopens.

Roman Libya

During the era of Roman rule in North Africa, which lasted over 500 years, Leptis Magna and Sabratha were among hundreds of North African cities absorbed into and developed by the empire. In the early days, Greece retained control of northeastern Libya, while the Romans took over the Punic settlements of Tripolitania, but it was not long before Rome had colonised Cyrenaica as well. Cultural distinctions persisted between the regions, which were different from each other and also very different from Rome itself. In Tripolitania, Punic continued to be the first language of much of the population, while Cyrenaica held on to the essence of its Greek heritage.

The citizens of Leptis and Sabratha embraced the Roman model of building and city improvements. Public life was central to the culture and grandiose buildings were required in order to live it to the highest standard. The monuments that survive attest to what were the important things in life, revealing themes as diverse as entertainment, worship, cleanliness, law, celebration and status. Triumphal arches, such as Leptis' Arch of Septimius Severus, were lavish manifestations of city pride, symbols of victory and success.

At the hub of any Roman city was the forum, a paved and colonnaded public square, which was the location of the *curia* (city hall) and much more besides. There was often a basilica (court of justice), alongside shops and bars. As people went about their daily lives, they were overlooked by huge statues of emperors and gods, some of whom had dedicated temples. Markets were also held in forums, although some cities had separate marketplaces. The one at Leptis is a fascinating example. Its reconstructed monuments include a stone tablet demonstrating a triple measuring system (Roman-Punic, Roman-Alexandrine and Greek).

Bathhouses played a central role in city life and the Hadrianic baths at Leptis were every bit as luxurious as the Great Baths in Rome. Sabratha's museum has on display a set of mosaic tiles that once adorned the theatre baths. Decorated with Latin notices or with images such as sandals and olive oil bottles, they provide an insight into the lifestyle of the city's inhabitants. One of the inscriptions translates simply as, 'washing is good for you'. Aside from their practical functions, the baths were places to socialise. Even

The magnificent ruins of the basilica at Leptis Magna

going to the toilet provided an occasion to chat, which people did while sitting in the ornamental public latrines often attached to the bathhouses.

Citizens of Roman cities loved entertainment, and theatres were among the most essential buildings. They were singular semicircular structures, often carved into the hillside. Sabratha and Leptis have the two largest surviving Roman theatres in Africa. The one at Sabratha is especially magnificent and has many restored original details, such as dramatic scenes carved into the front of the stage. Musical comedies were particularly popular.

Not all events were so light-hearted, however. The Romans also had a taste for public executions of an extremely cruel nature. Amphitheatres, differentiated from theatres by their completely circular structure, hosted bloodthirsty spectacles that saw prisoners forced to fight gladiators or wild animals.

The other main venue for public diversion was the circus, where horse and chariot races were the main attraction. Betting was popular and winning charioteers and horses were widely celebrated. Acrobats sometimes performed between races. The size of a city's amphitheatre and circus was another indication of status. Leptis Magna's circus was one of the biggest outside Rome, with room for 25,000 people. Its amphitheatre seated 16,000.

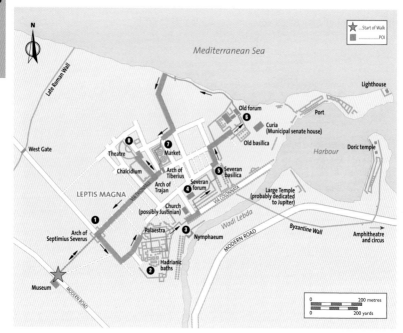

LEPTIS MAGNA

It is incredible to think, while standing in the midst of some of the most spectacular Roman ruins anywhere, that only 40 per cent of Leptis has actually been excavated. In the glory days of ancient Rome, it was the jewel in the crown of the empire's North African outposts. Although a Phoenician-Punic city was originally founded on the site as early as the 7th century BC, little remains of this settlement. The architecture of Leptis is almost entirely Roman in character. As an important trade centre between the Sahara and the sea, Leptis grew steadily in consequence. The city's main exports were olives, olive oil and the exotic animals from inland Africa desired by Rome for its entertainments.

By the end of Emperor Hadrian's reign (AD 117–38), Leptis was a grand city of limestone and marble, with a cutting-edge new aqueduct system to supply water to a grand bathhouse. The city's elevation to the super league, however, was triggered by Emperor Lucius Septimius Severus, who was born and bred in Leptis. During his reign (AD 193–211), some of the most impressive buildings in the city were constructed. Estimations have put the number of inhabitants during the city's heyday at around 80,000, making it the second most populated North African city after Carthage (Tunis).

Today, most of the monuments are concentrated in one large but easily navigable site. Only the amphitheatre and circus are located in a separate area, a short distance from the main site. In the main car park area you will find the entrance and ticket office, along with a few souvenir shops and stalls, a post and telephone office, a snack bar and public toilets (for which there is a minor charge). Visitors must be accompanied by a guide. Mahmud Tabib, who knows Leptis extremely well, deserves a mention here. *Tel: (092) 609 8085.*

Leptis can easily be visited from Tripoli, but some visitors use the nearby towns of Al Khums or Zliten as a base. Al Khums, 3km (1¾ miles) west of Leptis, took its name (which means 'one-fifth') from the percentage of income that inhabitants of Leptis had to give to Rome in tax.

Open: 8am–6pm. Admission & camera/ video charges.

Arch of Septimius Severus

Main site
Arch of Septimius Severus

As the nearest monument to the entrance, the iconic Arch of Septimius Severus serves as a magnificent introduction to Leptis. The original arch, built of limestone and marble in AD 203 in honour of the city's most famous son, sustained great damage over the centuries and has been painstakingly reconstructed by archaeologists. Posters and old photos on the inside of one of the pillars show what work has been done and what remains to be done. Today, although not yet finished, the restored arch looks impressively authentic.

It was designed as a triumphal arch, decorated with various representative sculptures and carvings. Many of the details you see on the arch are actually copies of the original carvings, which are now kept in the Tripoli or Leptis museums. Among the decorations are panels of sculpted figures, including Septimius Severus with his sons Caracalla and Geta, his second wife Julia Domna, and a number of deities. There are also scenes of military triumph, sacrifice and ceremony. The eagles spanning the inside of the dome are a classic Roman symbol for victory and power. Superstition has a place as well, in the form of eight pointed triangles perched atop the pillars. This design is found in various ancient structures throughout Libya and was thought to protect against evil.

Tripolitania: Leptis Magna and Sabratha

Hadrianic baths and *palaestra*

The Hadrianic baths and next-door *palaestra* (sports ground) together formed a complete leisure centre. Little remains of the *palaestra* except its distinctive outline and some marble columns. The type of marble used in these columns is called 'cipolin' (onion) because of its ringed greenish grain. The basic shape of the baths has been preserved but their original splendour can only be imagined. The artist's impression in room 8 of the museum is helpful. Fragments of the marble and mosaic floor remain, such as around the open-air swimming pool in the entrance hall. Beyond the *natatio* (entrance hall), the rooms are layered symmetrically from north to south. The *frigidarium* (cold room) is first, followed by the *tepidarium* (warm room) and finally the *caldarium* (hot room). The *tepidarium* is flanked on either side by a *laconica* (sauna). There are also small changing rooms to the side. The *frigidarium*, the largest and grandest room, was once ornamented with numerous statues. Some of these are now in the museums of Leptis and Tripoli. Outside, on the northeastern corner of the baths, is a square structure lined with marble benches with a hole in each individual seat. This was the *forica* (public latrines), one of the city's social spaces.

Market

The marketplace, scenically located overlooking the sea, is distinctive even

ROME'S FIRST AFRICAN EMPEROR

In AD 193, Septimius Severus, a Leptis-born Roman governor of Punic ancestry, seized imperial power in the wake of two emperors being murdered in quick succession. As emperor, he led a series of severe military campaigns, leading to his epithet, 'the grim African'. He married (as his second wife) Julia Domna from Syria and had two sons. The family travelled all over the empire, but Septimius never forgot the city of his childhood and Leptis benefited greatly from its connection to the wealthy emperor. With old buildings restored, an array of new monuments constructed and the infrastructure improved, Leptis entered a golden age.

by Leptis standards. Its restored monuments include two octagonal halls, where traders sold their wares. Extra stalls were set up in a portico encircling the halls, and some of the columns of the portico are standing today. There are the stone benches marked with rope-lines from where heavy produce was moved, and the copy of a stone measuring tablet with three different lengths, among other details. The original market was built in the earliest days of Leptis, and later rebuilt under Septimius Severus.

Nymphaeum and Via Colonnata

The *nymphaeum* was a temple to the nymphs. It once had a fountain and marble statues, but today the structure is indistinct. The ornate Via Colonnata (Colonnaded Street), one of the grandest and busiest thoroughfares in

The Hadrianic baths were a popular meeting place in Roman times

Leptis, ran for over 400m (435yds) from the *nymphaeum* to the port. Some of the columns, pedestals and arches are still standing.

Old forum and port areas

Although only vague traces remain of the old forum buildings, this area is worth a mention because it is the oldest part of Leptis, the heart of the original Punic settlement. There were once several temples here, as well as a basilica and *curia*. Look out for circular carvings on the ground, thought to have been used for game-playing. Along the coast to the east lies the port. Among the ruins that remain here are the foundation of the lighthouse, and some buildings that were part of the eastern quay.

Severan forum and basilica

These vast monuments are among Leptis' highlights, impressive for their scale and the abundance of original marble that remains. Covering an area of 100m by 60m (109yds by 66yds), the forum is an awe-inspiring space. Wandering through it, dwarfed by the marble columns that are still upright and negotiating those that are strewn across the ground, it is easy to imagine walking in the footsteps of the ancients. The forum, an open-air building, was originally watched over by a series of sculpted heads perched atop the columns. These representations of Medusa and the sea nymphs (Nereids) fell down, but some have been restored to their original eerie positions. Within the forum there was a stage for public announcements and a small shopping area.

The basilica is adjacent to the northeast side of the forum. It still has a feel of stern grandeur in keeping with its original incarnation as a judicial basilica. Look out for the elaborate marble pillars with their symbols representing Liber Pater and Hercules, the two main deities of Leptis. Marble panels with Latin inscriptions line the main hall.

Theatre

Yet another spectacular monument, this is one of ancient Rome's oldest surviving stone theatres. It consists of a semicircular fan of seats facing a stage with an ornate colonnaded façade and a dramatic backdrop of the Mediterranean Sea. Two statues on the stage represent the gods Liber Pater and Hercules, examples of the sculpture gallery that once practically covered the stage.

The well-preserved amphitheatre

Amphitheatre and circus

The seafront amphitheatre and circus are located about 3km (2 miles) east of the centre of Leptis Magna. Excavations of this site were not started until the 1970s. The circus is reached by walking through a passage from the amphitheatre. In Roman times, the amphitheatre was a busy, noisy, violent place of pitiless fighting, while the circus would have buzzed with the excitement of the races. Little remains of the circus except the foundations, which are interesting as markers of its scale. The amphitheatre, which was built into the hillside, is much more intact.
Open: 8am–6pm. Admission charge.

Museum

The museum is a short walk from the main site entrance. It merits a detour to learn more about Leptis and admire the statues found on the site. The museum has many rooms, which are well thought out and include explanations in English. Each room is themed according to the period the exhibits hail from or where they were found. There are also a few rooms concerned with general Libyan history or culture.

In the first room there is an artist's impression of how Leptis would have looked in its heyday, alongside exhibits relating to prehistoric Libya. Model reconstructions or paintings of particular Leptis buildings can be found throughout the museum. Other rooms deal with the city's Punic heritage and include Punic pottery found in excavations. Sculptural highlights include the collection of stunning marble statues in room 7, the subjects of which vary from the goddess Isis and the Emperor Marcus Aurelius to ordinary citizens of Leptis. The statues in room 12 are fascinating in a more eerie way, because they are all headless. It was common practice for sculptors to create a range of bodies to which they could add the heads of specific individuals at a later stage.
Open: Tue–Sun 8am–6pm. Admission & camera/video charges.

Detail of a Medusa head in the forum

Walk: Leptis Magna

This is a logical route around the main site of Leptis Magna and the seafront, which showcases the sheer scale of Libya's grandest ancient city and ensures that you see all the key monuments. These cover different time periods, from the Punic age to the Roman era, plus some later additions.

Allow 3 or 4 hours to walk and explore the sights on this 3km (2-mile) route.

Start at the site entrance (see map, p48). Follow the tree-lined path to a staircase and the Arch of Septimius Severus.

1 Arch of Septimius Severus

The arch (*see p49*) stands at a crossroads of the main streets through the city, the *cardo* (which runs north-south) and the *decumanus* (east-west). *Turn right under the arch. Follow the road to its end and turn left. At the corner, look back for a great view of the arch. At the end of the road, turn right and double round to the right through the* palaestra *to the baths.*

2 Hadrianic baths

The first area you come to is the *natatio* (entrance hall). The rest of the baths are layered to the south behind this (*see p50*).
After a circuit of the baths, exit on the northeastern side, with the natatio *on your left, and pass through the latrines to get back to the* palaestra. *Turn right onto the path.*

3 *Nymphaeum* and Via Colonnata

At the end of the path leading out of the *palaestra*, you will reach a square featuring a tall semicircular temple, the *nymphaeum*, from where the Colonnaded Street starts (*see pp50–51*). *Facing the temple, turn left along the road towards the sea. Look out for a section of wall on the left, after which there is an entrance to the forum.*

4 Severan forum

As you enter over a raised step from the Colonnaded Street, you will see a staircase and platform to the left, which are the ruins of the temple to the imperial Severan dynasty. The rest of the forum stretches out in front of you (*see p52*).
The entrance to the basilica is at the far (northeastern) end of the forum.

5 Severan basilica

This rectangular two-storey building still contains many of its original features (*see p52*). There is a staircase which still gives access to the upper level, although you should always check with your guide before climbing up.

Exiting at the northwestern corner, follow a cleared track to the Byzantine Gate. Turn right here and you will soon find yourself in the old forum.

6 Old forum and seafront

Little remains of the old forum, apart from a few scattered remnants (*see p51*). If you walk straight through and follow a sandy path curving to the left, you will reach the seafront. Following the path, you come to three abandoned marble columns lying by the sea.

Take the path leading back inland from the columns and continue straight down to reach the market.

7 Market and monumental arches

The marketplace, which overlooks the sea, is particularly photogenic and merits leisurely exploration (*see p50*). Exit on the southern side to see the monumental limestone arches of Trajan and Tiberius on the Via Trionfale.

Take a detour to the right at the second arch. Go past the chalcidium *building and continue to the theatre.*

8 Theatre

End your walk with one of the best views in Tripolitania, looking out over the Mediterranean from the top seats of the theatre.

Retrace your steps back past the chalcidium *to the Arch of Trajan. Turn right and return to the Arch of Septimius Severus.*

Walk: Leptis Magna

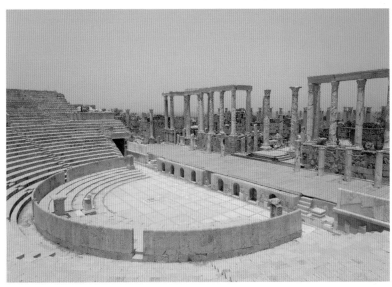

A great location for the theatre at Leptis Magna

SABRATHA

Sabratha was first founded in the 4th century BC by Punic settlers (of Phoenician origin but from Carthage), primarily as a trading port. They planted olive and fruit trees and exported olive oil, wine and fruit to Europe. The city was given its first makeover in the 2nd century BC, when Greek settlers appeared on the scene. It was damaged by an earthquake in the 1st century AD and rebuilt under the Romans. Sabratha thrived until the 3rd century, but fell into decline following the major earthquake of 365 and the fall of the Roman Empire.

Sabratha has always been overshadowed in some ways by the bigger and more obviously impressive Leptis, which is a shame as this seafront city is actually one of the most charming classical sites in Libya. In fact, Sabratha and Leptis complement each other well by showing different aspects of the ancient world. At Sabratha, remains of the original Punic settlement and Hellenistic touches from when the

The theatre at Sabratha has undergone much restoration

city was inhabited by the Greek settlers can be seen alongside the Roman ruins, so it shows the layers of occupation better than Leptis.

Excavations and restorations at Sabratha were started by the Italians early in the 20th century and further work has been done over the years, right up to the present day. Around 30 per cent of the site has been excavated. One tour guide who specialises in Sabratha is the very knowledgeable Abdelmajid Elhindi. *Tel: (092) 720 1647.*

Museum

Sabratha's museum was built in 1930 by the Italians and houses an array of architectural treasures. Despite its small size, this is arguably one of the most interesting site museums in Libya and an essential stop on any tour of Sabratha. It has three wings, arranged around a courtyard, although the western wing was closed for renovations at the time of writing. Sabratha was known for its mosaics and the museum has some stunning examples of these.

The central wing is dedicated to huge mosaic panels taken from the Basilica of Justinian (*see below*). These beautiful works are rich in symbolism. The one covering the floor, which includes a peacock, doves and a phoenix, has been interpreted as an allegory of the soul. The eastern wing has more mosaics, this time excavated from houses, plus frescoes, paintings and sculptures. One of the highlights here is an intricate

Statue of an emperor at Sabratha Museum

mosaic depicting a lion, a panther and a chariot carrying Bacchus (the god of wine and a very important figure), Ariadne, Minette and Pan. The delicate frescoes and paintings are lovely, while some of the sculptures have been brilliantly well preserved.

Public buildings

Among Sabratha's churches are two grand basilicas: the Judicial Basilica and the Basilica of Justinian. The **Judicial Basilica** functioned mainly as a court during the Roman era before being converted into a church by the Byzantines. The **Basilica of Justinian** was purpose-built in the 6th century as a church, although it contains features from earlier periods, such as a column

The enormous Mausoleum of Bes

of the excavated residential areas is located between the museum and the entrance to the main site. Pottery of four different styles, from Rome, Greece, Carthage and Libya, has been found in some of the houses. The reconstructed Mausoleum of Bes (or Mausoleum B) is one of the most idiosyncratic monuments in Sabratha. At nearly 24m (79ft) tall, it towers over the surrounding ruins. The figures at the top are Hercules and the Punic god Bes, who was believed to be the protector of the sleeping and the dead.

Seaward Baths and old port area

The Seaward Baths is one of the loveliest places in Sabratha. Its seafront location frames to great effect the wonderfully intact mosaic and marble floor. To the west of the Seaward Baths is the old port area, where you can see an olive-oil press and storage cellar on the beach. The street leading from here was logically named 'Oil Press Street', in keeping with a general theme which saw other roads being given names like 'Wine Street'.

Temples

Sabratha had seven temples, of which three were Hellenistic and four Roman. The Hellenistic temples had sandstone columns and limestone floors, while the Roman equivalents had columns of cipolin marble and were also paved with marble. Unfortunately, relatively few of the original features of Sabratha's

decorated with carvings of acanthus leaves. Some of the dazzling mosaics in the museum originated from this basilica. Between the two basilicas lie the forum and *curia* (senate house). Both are characterised by the columns of grey granite which are among their surviving features.

Punic Mausoleum of Bes and old residential quarters

Excavations at Sabratha have unearthed houses, as well as public buildings. One

temples remain. The first temple you come to is the South Forum Temple, or 'Southern Temple to an Unknown Divinity'. Although little remains of the original building structure, the marble floor is fairly intact. Other temples were dedicated to Liber Pater, Serapis, Isis and Emperor Antoninus Pius. The last, called the Antonine Temple, sits by a fountain square, where one of a number of fountains remains. Next to the fountain is a statue of Flavius Tullus, an eminent citizen who established an aqueduct system.

Theatre

The theatre is wonderful, a highlight not only of Sabratha, but of classical Libya in general. In contrast to the theatre at Leptis, rebuilding works here centred on the stage and the façade behind it, restoring them to their former glory. There are so many intricate details in the stage and façade that the theatre alone merits long exploration. Sculpted marble panels set in niches enliven the front of the stage. They depict an eclectic variety of scenes from popular plays and mythology, as well as personifications of the cities of Sabratha and Rome. The carved dolphins at the side of the stage are eye-catching as well. The theatre was used in the 3rd and 4th centuries. It is in use again now for annual Revolution Day celebrations.

Intricately carved marble at Sabratha theatre

Theatre quarter

Near the theatre, the Theatre Baths gave patrons a handy venue for a relaxing pre- or post-performance soak. Another complex, the Baths of Oceanus, is also located nearby. Some sections of mosaic remain in the ruins, although the most interesting are in the museum.

OTHER ATTRACTIONS OF TRIPOLITANIA
Villa Sileen

In the Roman heyday of Leptis Magna, the country retreats of rich citizens stretched along the coast in both directions. Villa Sileen is the only one left. The villa was opened to the public a few years ago, but it seems it was actually still in need of renovations and at the time of writing it had been closed again. Hopefully it will be reopened soon, so that visitors can enjoy one of the most beautiful collections of mosaics in Tripolitania. In the main section of the villa, the floors of every room are adorned with mosaics and there are yet more in the side (eastern) wing, which housed the all-important baths.

Janzur museum

Janzur is a small town 13km (8 miles) to the west of Tripoli. For anyone interested in Byzantine antiquity, the museum merits a quick visit, probably on the journey to Sabratha. Alongside a range of small and varied artefacts, the museum houses an intriguing Byzantine tomb, which was found locally.

WHO'S WHO OF GODS AND GODDESSES

Greek name	Roman name	Associations	Symbols
Aphrodite	Venus	Love, lust, beauty	Sceptre, myrtle, dove
Apollo	Apollo	Music, archery, the arts, truth, prophecy, the sun	Bow, lyre, laurel
Artemis	Diana	Hunting, forests, fertility/virginity, wild animals, the moon	Bow, deer
Athena	Minerva	Wisdom	Owl, olive tree
Demeter	Ceres	Fertility, harvest	Sceptre, torch, corn
Dionysus	Bacchus	Wine, festivities, merriment	Grapevine, ivy
Hades	Pluto	The underworld	Two-pronged spear
Hera	Juno	Women, marriage, childbirth	Sceptre, peacock
Heracles	Hercules	Champion of the gods, strength, sports	Lion, club
Hermes	Mercury	Messenger of the gods	Winged boots
Persephone (Kore)	Proserpina	Spring	Pomegranate
Poseidon	Neptune	Sea, earthquakes	Trident
Zeus	Jupiter	King of the gods	Thunderbolt, eagle, oak

Open: Tue–Sun 10am–6pm.
Admission charge.

Zuara

Zuara is situated 40km (25 miles) west of Sabratha and 60km (37 miles) east of the border with Tunisia. The beaches around this seaside Berber town are picturesque and there is an excellent tourist village nearby (*see p167*), which is popular with Libyan families in the summer. There is also an annual festival in August (*see p18*).

Ghirza

Ghirza is a long way from any other sites or cities, but it has a place among the ancient sites of Libya for its 3rd-century Romanised Libyan monuments. The old settlement is notable particularly for its detailed stonework, which includes tombs, temples and fortified farms. There are examples of these in Jamahiriya Museum in Tripoli (galleries 1 and 5, *see pp37–9*) and in the Leptis museum (*see p53*).
Open site. Free admission.

Tripolitania: Leptis Magna and Sabratha

A bust of Jupiter (Zeus) at Sabratha Museum

Cyrenaica

This northeastern corner of Libya boasts a surprisingly temperate climate and green landscape. The rolling hills of the Jebel al-Akhdar region protect the narrow coastal strip from the desert. Cyrenaica's ruined cities add to the region's distinctiveness, serving as monuments to the ancient Greek influence here. In ancient Greek times, five cities were established in Cyrenaica, collectively known as the Pentapolis: Cyrene, Apollonia, Ptolemais (Tolmeita), Teuchira (Tocra) and Eusperides (near Benghazi).

Cyrenaica, with its plentiful agricultural land, thrived as a highly valuable outpost for Greece. The degree of autonomy enjoyed by the cities varied over the centuries, but Cyrenaica has always had a distinct identity. Cultural elements that marked it out as unique included the worship of a hybrid Greek-Libyan deity (Zeus Ammun). The region was linked with Egypt at various points in its history from the time of Alexander the Great to the

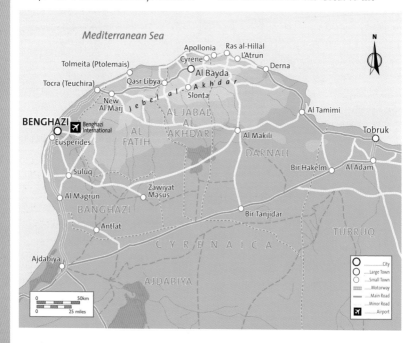

The double harbour at Benghazi

Islamic era. More recently, Cyrenaica was at the forefront of Libyan resistance to foreign oppression. The rebellions against the Ottoman and Italian occupations were concentrated here and the worst horrors of the latter were exacted on the Cyrenaicans. Half the region's population were among the tens of thousands of Libyans who died in conflict or in concentration camps.

Today, its past shaken off but not forgotten, the region remains characterised by its cultural and geographical individuality. The most impressive sites are located in the north-central area. Cyrene, the principal city of the Pentapolis, is a fascinating window on the past, as are the smaller cities of Apollonia and Tolmeita. Highlights of different kinds are provided by the mosaics at Qasr

Libya and the landscapes around Wadi al-Kuf and Ras al-Hillal. For most visitors to Cyrenaica, the first port of call is the modern city of Benghazi, Libya's second city.

Benghazi

Although not in the same league as Tripoli, Benghazi is pleasant, has interesting sights, several nice places to sleep and eat, a scenic double harbour and a cooling sea breeze. What it does not have, despite lying on the site of an ancient Greek city, is the visible history found elsewhere along the coast. The first settlement in the area was Eusperides. Little is known about Eusperides except that it was probably founded in the 6th century BC and was believed to be a mythical site, namely the location of the garden of

Benghazi's waterfront promenade with the old lighthouse in the background

Hesperides, where golden apples grew. Several centuries later the settlers deserted Eusperides and built a new city nearby, named Berenice after a Cyrenaican princess turned Egyptian queen. Benghazi was built over the ruins of Berenice. The fortunes of the city continued to ebb and flow over the centuries. It was particularly badly damaged by bombings during World War II and again in 1986, when the USA attacked Libya over alleged involvement in international terrorism. Much of the city remains in need of renovation, but the interesting mix of architectural styles is apparent nonetheless. Many of the streets have whitewashed arched walkways and a generally Italianate feel.

Acacus House

Undoubtedly one of the unique arts attractions in Libya and one of Benghazi's most interesting sights, this is the work of one artist, wood sculptor Ali Al-Wakwak. In Libya there is a tradition of artists exhibiting in their houses and Ali is an example of this. His idiosyncratic house is filled to the brim with impressive wooden sculptures. *Sharia Elaneizi. Tel: 091 380 1741. Free admission.*

Souq al-Jreed

Souq al-Jreed is a long, bustling covered market selling everything from gold jewellery to assorted cheap goods and great snacks like falafel, fresh fruit juices and milkshakes.

Cyrene

In the peak era of Greek rule, Cyrene was a magnificent city. A long and turbulent history saw it ruled in turn by the original Greek settlers, Alexander the Great, the Ptolemaic Empire of Egypt and the Romans, before being severely damaged in the Jewish Revolt of the 1st century AD. Cyrene was restored to glory under Emperor Hadrian, only to be destroyed again over the following centuries by earthquakes and finally the Islamic invasion.

Today, although much of the vast site remains unexcavated, enough has been done to evoke travelling back in time. Cyrene's hilly setting is unique among the major ancient cities of Libya and the landscape is beautiful. The shade of the trees, the scent of wild herbs and the buzzing of bees add to the site's almost mythical appeal. Honey and herbs are sold at the roadside along with postcards and souvenirs and there are a few cafés. Two tour guides worth mentioning for their extensive knowledge of Cyrene (and Apollonia) are Mohammed Bo Sharit and Ali M Adam.

Open: May–Sept 7.30am–6pm; Oct–Apr 8am–5pm. Admission & camera/ video charges.

Agora

The agora served as marketplace and general public square. The most eye-catching and unique monument here

Cyrene

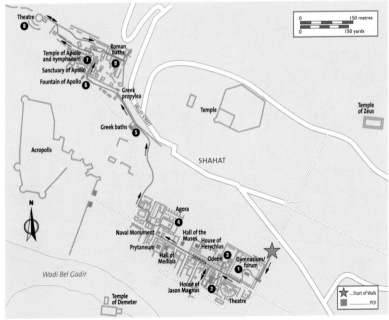

is the **Naval Monument**. This reconstructed marble statue of a ship was originally built to celebrate a marine victory in the 3rd century BC. It features beautifully carved details, such as a female figure, dolphins, and tridents of Neptune/Poseidon.

Gymnasium area and houses

Nearest to the site entrance are the ruins of the city centre, among which has been excavated the gymnasium, built in the 2nd century BC to host sporting events and later turned into a forum by the Romans. Running along the southwest edge of the gymnasium are the remnant wall and columns of the Skyrota, the main road through the ancient Greek city. Also in this area are a couple of small theatres. The odeon, used for musical performances, is particularly atmospheric. One of

Cyrene's signature monuments is the **House of Jason Magnus**, a high priest and eminent resident during the 2nd century AD. Its highlight is a beautiful 'Four Seasons' mosaic.

Museum

The single room forming Cyrene's museum is absolutely packed with Greek and Roman statues and other artefacts. Signs are translated into English and Italian. Many of the statues are remarkably well preserved, as is a collection of inscribed stone tablets, still amazingly legible. Look out for the funerary statues, unique to Cyrenaica and some of the oldest pieces in the museum. Also noteworthy is the huge stone sphinx sitting atop a column at the front of the room. This once overlooked Cyrene from a vantage point of 6.2m (20½ft). Other relics remain sadly

Cyrene's Temple of Zeus

incomplete, like the huge fingers displayed in a cabinet. They were part of a massive statue of Zeus, the rest of which is missing. Security issues have been a major issue at this and other sites throughout Libya. There are a few mosaics, including a depiction of Theseus and the Minotaur, one of a satyr and a nymph, and an intricate design of the Three Graces. The last is missing many pieces, but the intact sections showcase the delicate Hellenistic design of the tiny marble and glass tiles. *Open: Sat–Thur. Closed: Fri.*

Necropolis

There are more than 2,000 tombs distributed across the countryside around Cyrene. The ones you can see from the road as you approach the site from the coastal direction are particularly eye-catching. They are carved into the cliff, facing out over the hills and sea, and almost look like natural, albeit eerie, features of the rock. The oldest tombs date from the 6th century BC. After the Greeks, they were used by the Romans and Byzantines. Some of them had an additional function in Roman times as storage rooms and later many were used as shelter by nomads.

Sanctuary of Apollo

Situated on a ledge in the side of the mountain is the collection of buildings that formed the spiritual heart of the city. Some of the monuments have been reconstructed, while others have only fragments remaining. The *nymphaeum* (sacred fountain) has been carefully restored and has symbolic carvings of lions. The nearby **Temple of Apollo** was originally one of the oldest temples in Cyrene. Although its surviving sections date from the Roman era, they were designed in the Greek style. Other interesting features include the ancient Greek monumental gateway and the Roman baths, which still contain some of the original mosaic flooring and marble columns.

Temple of Zeus

Secluded in a pine forest to the east of the main site, the lofty Temple of Zeus is one of Cyrene's marvels. At eight columns wide by seventeen long, it is bigger than the Parthenon in Athens. Restoration works are being carried out by Italian archaeologists, but enough has already been done to enable visitors to wander among the towering columns. This was a highly sacred place, used at different times to honour Zeus, Jupiter (under the Romans) and Zeus Ammun.

Theatre

Even in the context of Cyrene's stunning location and atmospheric character, the theatre stands out. The view from here is simply fantastic and the scale of the semicircular structure carved into the hillside is impressive. It was built during the Greek era and modified by the Romans.

Walk: Cyrene

Ancient Cyrene is spread out across a large site but, apart from the Temple of Zeus, most of the monuments are located in the agora area and the Sanctuary of Apollo. This scenic walking route takes you from one to the other, highlighting some of the most interesting monuments along the way.

Allow about 3 hours to meander this 2km (1¼-mile) route.

Start at the site entrance (see map, p65). Go straight ahead and you will come to the signposted gymnasium on your right.

1 Gymnasium/forum and Skyrota

Little remains of the structure of the gymnasium except the two imposing entrance gates (*see p66*). On the southwest of the gymnasium (left of the gateways) is the start of the Skyrota, once the main road through the city.
Follow the path of the Skyrota, and turn left into the House of Jason Magnus.

2 House of Jason Magnus

Most of the splendid mosaics and statues from this private house (*see p66*) are now in the museum. However, you can still see the outlines of the rooms, marble floors, a few statues and a 'Four Seasons' mosaic.
Opposite the house, on the other side of the main path, is a tunnelled back entrance to the odeon.

3 Odeon

The odeon is small but well preserved, making quite an impression as you emerge into the daylight from the tunnelled entrance.
Exit through the tunnel, turn right, back onto the main thoroughfare, and follow it along to the Agora. There are several labelled monuments along the way.

4 Agora

The agora is basically an open square dotted with monuments, the most interesting being the Naval Monument on the eastern side (*see pp65–6*).
From the northwestern corner of the Agora a path ambles downhill to the Sanctuary of Apollo. The view from this path is an attraction in itself. Near the bottom of the path, on the left of the steps down, is a sign for the 'Greek Hellenistic Bath'.

5 Greek baths

Carved into the mountainside, the structure of the ancient baths remains intact. This stone cavern lined with seats is also a unique place to cool off briefly on a hot day.

Continue down the path to the sanctuary. You will see an entrance with four columns, the ancient Greek propylea *(monumental gateway). Turn left and follow the path to the Fountain of Apollo, under the cliff opposite the sanctuary.*

6 Fountain of Apollo

The Fountain of Apollo was constructed around a natural spring and used as a bathing place during the Greek period. Today, the deep pools are home to frogs and dragonflies.

Enter the sanctuary. In the centre, roughly opposite the Fountain of Apollo, is the Temple of Apollo.

7 Temple of Apollo and *nymphaeum*

The first monument you come to is the *nymphaeum* (sacred fountain). The temple is behind it. Look out for the ancient (6th-century BC) limestone and marble altar, monumental at over 20m (65ft) long.

Walk to the west, a short distance outside the sanctuary, along the edge of the plateau, to reach the theatre.

8 Theatre

Climb to the highest seats of the theatre (*see p67*) for a panoramic view across the coastal plain.

Return to the sanctuary and walk straight through. The Roman baths are on the eastern edge, by the northern gate exit.

9 Roman baths

As you walk out through the Roman baths, you can see some final Cyrene mosaics and marble columns. In the *frigidarium* (cold room), there is a Latin dedication to Hadrian, who restored the baths during his reign.

A view of the sea and the Necropolis from the Sanctuary of Apollo

Greek Cyrenaica

The first Greek settlers arrived on the shores of northeastern Libya in the early 7th century BC. They were from the island of Thera (now Santorini) and were relocating according to advice received from the oracle at Delphi, to leave behind the power struggles and agricultural shortages plaguing their homeland. The story of their decision was immortalised by a 'Founders' Decree' inscribed on a stone tablet in Cyrene. The tablet is now in the museum as one of a collection of large tablets recording important city information, providing fascinating insight into the city's history.

A naval monument at Cyrene

Cyrene had humble beginnings as a default site, to which the Greek invaders were led by a local tribe wanting to divert them from their own land. However, it grew to become one of the most important cities on the ancient Greek map. All the cities of the Pentapolis went from strength to strength, with the capital as the jewel in the crown. Greek Cyrenaica was in its heyday in the 4th century BC. The land around Cyrene was ideal for agriculture and the city became wealthy, even finding itself in a position to rescue Greece from famine by donating huge quantities of corn. This export is also recorded on one of the stone tablets in the museum.

Among the many crops that were cultivated on this rich land was an indigenous plant called silphium, which became almost revered in Cyrenaica and beyond. It was believed to have extensive properties. In addition to being harvested as a medicinal ingredient, it is also known to have been used to flavour food and possibly as an aphrodisiac. Silphium was one of the emblems of Cyrenaica and was represented on local coins. It is now extinct, although some of the plants still growing in the

Ancient Greek underground baths

region resemble it a little. Drawings can be seen in some museums and there are ancient carved representations on the columns of Al Bayda's Temple of Aesculapius (the god of healing).

Cyrene's agricultural richness was mirrored in the cultural domain. It had many schools and was home to several renowned individuals across diverse fields including philosophy, mathematics, astronomy and music. A happiness-centred school of philosophy was developed in the city. Cultural pursuits were important to the citizens of Cyrenaica. Cyrene itself had five theatres to stage plays, music concerts and political speeches. There was even a women-only theatre and an annual women's celebration, held in the Sanctuary of Demeter and Kore. The general spirituality of the ancient citizens of Cyrenaica is evident from the number of temples that were built and the number of deities that were worshipped. Cyrene's Sanctuary of Apollo was a spiritual place of baths, fountains and temples dedicated to different gods and goddesses.

In more earthly matters, Cyrenaican horses were extremely popular for their speed and strength. In a culture that prized chariot races as one of the top forms of entertainment and sport, this must have been an extra accolade for the region. Sport was also a significant aspect of public life. Look out for the carvings of Heracles and Hermes on the gymnasium columns in Cyrene. These symbols of strength and speed watched over the sporting events.

Cyrenaica

Apollonia

Apollonia was originally the port for Cyrene, but it also became an important centre in its own right, especially during the Byzantine era. The Byzantines changed the city's name to Susa, which meant 'safe here', and constructed five churches. Today, the site is known again as Apollonia, while the modern town just outside its boundaries is called Susa. The ruins here are heavily weighted towards the Byzantine period, with just a few reminders of Greek and Roman Apollonia, such as the Roman baths next to the Central Church.

Due to the city's seafront location, much has been swallowed by the Mediterranean, including the city wall, harbour and marketplace. Statues and boats have been discovered in underwater excavations and a large

THE MYTH OF CYRENE

The principal character in the story of Cyrenaica's foundation was an action heroine. The myth tells how a lion was terrorising the region until the Greek nymph Cyrene strangled it. Cyrene's act of bravery achieved both safety and legitimacy for the colony, the land having been saved by one of its own. Meanwhile, the heroine had also attracted the attentions of Apollo, who fell in love with her and whisked her away in a golden chariot. The couple were honoured through the naming of the city of Cyrene and the Sanctuary of Apollo. With their son Aristaeus, destined to be the god of bee-keeping among other rural pursuits, they became a godly family, inextricably linked to Cyrenaica.

Greek ship still remains under the sea. The section on dry land is small, but significant. The site entrance is on the western edge and the ruins run from west to east, closely shadowing the coast. This is farmland, so you may see

The Western Church at Apollonia

The Greek theatre by the beach

sheep roaming the ruins. Also note the pottery and marble shards just lying around, mainly turned up by moles. *Open: May–Sept 7.30am–7pm; Oct–Apr 8am–5pm. Admission & camera/ video charges.*

Beach

There are monuments right down to the shore. The large circular holes in the rocks were a public larder, used to store olive oil, fish and fish oil. The beach wall is ornamented with pieces of ancient pottery and has a visible cistern and aqueduct at its base.

Byzantine ruins

The nearest monument to the entrance is the **Western Church**. It features Roman and Byzantine-style columns. The ones with a greenish hue, called 'cipolin' (onion) columns because of their layered grain, are Roman. The white ones are Byzantine. The **Central Church** has columns of various shapes and sizes, many of them inscribed with the Coptic cross. It also boasts a pristine little marble baptistery. The **Eastern Church**, once the largest church in the region, still has some of its massive marble columns and some mosaics. Slightly inland is the **Duke's Palace**, which was once a very grand residence. Many of the walls and some additional features, including a staircase and arched doorways, are still standing.

Theatre

Originally constructed during the Greek period, the theatre was enlarged by the Romans. It is on the far east of the site and its seafront setting, with the waves crashing just behind the stage, is wonderfully atmospheric.

Drive: Around Apollonia and Cyrene

This tour features both historical and geographical highlights of northern Cyrenaica. It takes in some stunning scenery, as well as including the sites of Apollonia and Cyrene and scattered monuments in the nearby countryside.

The tour covers just over 100km (62 miles) and needs to be spread over 2 days as there is much to see.

The starting point for the route is Apollonia. However, you could base yourself near Cyrene and reverse the order of the tour. From Apollonia, follow the coastal road east. After about 20km (12½ miles), the road sweeps round to the right and a stunning vista of a crescent bay comes into view. Take a left turn off the main road to get to the church.

1 Ras al-Hillal church

Ras al-Hillal has one of the most beautiful coastal locations in Libya, plus an ancient Byzantine church. There is also a small beach to the east of the church.

Return to the main road. Take a left turn, passing the village of Ras al-Hillal (which is about 3km/2 miles further on from the church). Follow the road for about 10km (6 miles), then take a left turn when you come to a village on the right. At the end of this road turn left. There is a dirt track to L'Atrun's Western Church after about 150m (165yds).

2 L'Atrun churches

L'Atrun's Western Church overlooks the Mediterranean. The Eastern Church is a short walk to the east.

Return to Ras al-Hillal village (a drive of about 10km/6 miles) and take the left turn leading up into the mountains behind the village. The road zigzags up for about 7km (4¼ miles) before reaching a plateau. Follow the road as it bends to the left. The mausoleums are set back from the road on the left side.

3 Greek mausoleums and waterfall

The Greek mausoleums were built around the 4th century BC. Near some of the tombs, ancient chariot tracks are visible in the ground. Unfortunately, graffiti has blighted the visual effect of the tombs. On the journey up to the tombs, look out for the small waterfall threading its way down the forested slope to the sea. It comes into view about 2km (1¼ miles) from the top of the winding road.

Return back down the hill to Ras al-Hillal and then on to Apollonia.

4 Apollonia

The ancient harbour city of Apollonia (*see pp72–3*) is a good site to visit in the afternoon. It takes on an especially atmospheric feel as the sun begins to sink, and its compact size allows for an easy stroll to round off the day.
Continue the route the same day if you are going to stay near Cyrene, or the next morning if you are staying a second night in Apollonia. Take the main road heading west from Apollonia. Very soon you will come to a junction. Take the road into the hills, not the coast road. The road quickly begins to climb. About 18km (11 miles) from

Apollonia, take the right turn on the horseshoe bend.

5 Necropolis

The incredible necropolis of Cyrene, numerous individual tombs carved into the hillside, comes into view after the bend (*see p67*).
Within a couple of kilometres you will reach Cyrene, 600m (2,000ft) above sea level.

6 Cyrene

Your first glimpse of Cyrene will be the Sanctuary of Apollo. It is a sight sure to impress. You need to devote the best part of a day to exploring Cyrene (*see pp65–9*).
Retrace the route back to Apollonia.

Drive: Around Apollonia and Cyrene

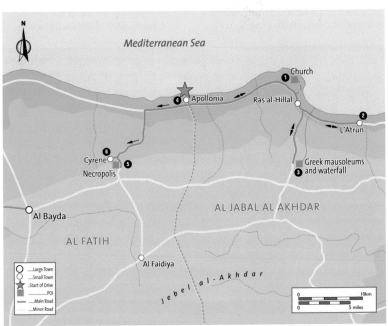

Tolmeita (Ptolemais)

Only about 10 per cent of the ancient city of Ptolemais, now called Tolmeita, has been excavated, but the compact site has much to offer. Its monuments showcase the difference in architectural styles between the Greeks and the Romans. There are several examples of how the Romans transformed existing Hellenistic buildings. In a modern postscript to this tradition of layering, the Italians built a village on top of the buried ancient city. Today, the residents have relocated nearby and these houses stand empty. There are also three Italian fortresses in the area and good beaches, which provide a pleasant venue for a picnic. The ticket office, museum and a small restaurant with public toilets are all located in the car park. Among the guides who specialise in tours of Tolmeita, Abdusalam Bazama deserves a particular mention. He was involved in the excavations and planted some of the trees around the site.

Open: 7.30am–5pm. Admission & camera/video charges.

Colonnaded Palace

The most significant monument along the second *cardo* (north-south road) is the Colonnaded Palace, or Villa of Columns. It has sections of black-and-white patterned mosaic on the floor and some fragments of marble and bronze.

Museum

Tolmeita's museum houses an impressive collection of mosaics, statues and tomb covers. The mosaics are a particular highlight. Like the monuments, they show an intriguing

The underground cisterns at Tolmeita were the biggest in North Africa

Columns and pillars feature often in Tolmeita's architecture

transition between ancient styles. An example is a stunning Medusa head detail from the Hellenistic period, which is embedded in a larger Roman mosaic.

Southern area and cisterns

East of the Colonnaded Palace is a Greek odeon, which was turned into a swimming pool by the Romans. A little uphill from the odeon is the agora (marketplace), which became a Roman forum. Although some interesting features of these structures remain, the real highlight of Tolmeita is underground. The cisterns, which collected rain and spring water, are reached via a staircase in the agora. Take care not to fall down the shafts. Built by the Greeks and extended by the Romans, these became the biggest cisterns in North Africa, with a staggering capacity of 8 million litres (over 1¾ million gallons). Now that they are empty, and lit by shards of sunlight, their impressive structure can be admired.

Southwestern area

Little remains of Tolmeita's Monumental Road (*decumanus*, east-west road) except a few column bases. It was once adorned with arched pillared walkways. To the southwest of the crossroads of the *decumanus* and the first *cardo* (north-south road) is a Byzantine church and a little further on is the **Villa of the Four Seasons**. The villa dates to the Roman period and was covered in mosaics, including a stunning and intact 'Four Seasons' mosaic, now in the museum.

Qasr Libya

The quiet village of Qasr Libya is home to a real gem: a set of perfectly preserved Byzantine mosaics. In 1957, Libyan dam workers stumbled upon two Byzantine churches adorned with extraordinary floor mosaics from the 6th century AD. The most fascinating of the mosaics are 50 square panels that were lifted from the floor of the Eastern Church and are now in the museum. In the ruins of the Eastern Church (about 100m/110yds east of the museum) are 50 symmetrical square gaps in the floor left by the panels. Opposite the museum is the cross-shaped Western Church, which still has a mosaic on its floor. Next door to the museum there is also a small Turkish fort.

Museum

The 50 mosaic panels are displayed around the museum walls and there is a larger mosaic, of a Nile scene, on the floor. The panels are numbered and briefly described in Arabic and English. Panel 23 has an inscription recording that the mosaics were laid in the church in what would have been AD 539. Subject matter ranges from natural scenes to early Christian ideology. All the mosaics are skilfully rendered yet

deceptively simplistic. Cyrenaica retained cultural links to Greece until the end of the Byzantine era and this Hellenistic influence can be seen in the size of the ceramic pieces. Animal mosaics include the descriptively labelled 'duck sitting on a curiously humped crocodile'. River scenes are numerous and include images of lotus flowers, waterfowl, fish and a merman. The gods of the Four Rivers of Paradise also appear. Some of the panels feature buildings, such as a turreted castle and a church. Panels 48 and 49 have been considered to be of special significance, due to their Pharos lighthouse images. *Open: daily 7.30am–5pm. Admission & camera/video charges.*

Tocra (Teuchira)

Tocra is the smallest of the region's ancient sites and it does not have the impressively preserved ruins of its neighbours. However, it does have an interesting Turkish-Italian fort, with intact stairs which you can climb to reach the upper level for lovely views over the sea. The traces of the ancient city are mostly located to the west of the fort (actually outside the entrance gate). Little remains of the structures, which include churches, a Greek gymnasium,

Panels 26 to 30 of the Qasr Libya mosaics

An Italian tank outside Rommel's bunker at Tobruk

Roman baths and tombs, but there are some preserved details. Perhaps of most interest are the ancient Greek inscriptions on several of the ruins. There is also a small museum near the fort (separate admission charge).
Open: May–Sept 7.30am–7.30pm; Oct–Apr 7.30am–5pm. Admission & camera/video charges.

Tobruk

The remote outpost of Tobruk is a town of commemoration. It was the site of major battles during World War II. There are five main World War II sites, four cemeteries and the Fig Tree, which was an Australian field hospital. The two largest cemeteries, **Knightsbridge** (at Acroma, 20km/12^1/$_2$ miles west of Tobruk) and **Tobruk Commonwealth War Cemetery** (6km/3^3/$_4$ miles south of

the Tobruk town centre), contain over 6,000 graves between them. A number of nationalities are represented here, including the UK, New Zealand, South Africa, Australia, India, Poland and Canada. The cemeteries have been beautifully maintained by the **Commonwealth War Graves Commission** (*UK tel: (+44 1628) 507 200. www.cwgc.org*). A peaceful, green feel is created in this harshest of landscapes by flowering plants and trellised alcoves with benches. The **French Cemetery**, 80km (50 miles) southeast of town, is smaller, but has a similar layout. The **German Cemetery**, which is right near the centre of town, is very different. Built in the style of a fort, it has towering mosaic slabs, inscribed with the soldiers' names, all around the inner walls.

Mosaics

The art form of mosaic-making was developed by the ancient Greeks, who constructed the earliest decorative mosaics from differently coloured pebbles. By the 2nd century BC, the craft was evolving and gaining in popularity. Mosaic artists had started using *tesserae* (small purpose-cut squares). These were mainly cut from natural stone, which dictated the colour palette, although glass also began to feature in some mosaics. Some of the *tesserae* were absolutely tiny and the images and patterns depicted were often exquisitely detailed.

The Romans learnt the craft from the Greeks and adapted it to suit their style. Mosaic floors became widespread during the Roman era,

Mosaic of a satyr and nymph at Cyrene Museum

although only in the villas of the rich, where they were must-have decorations, and in showpiece public buildings like bathhouses. The Byzantines also adored mosaics and accorded high status to the art form, decorating the walls and sometimes even ceilings of their churches with mosaic panels. They favoured the use of glass *tesserae* in a rainbow of colours, sometimes even with gold or silver leaf added.

Libya has a wealth of antique mosaics from the Hellenistic, Roman and Byzantine periods. Although the colossal earthquakes that caused so much destruction to the coastal cities took their toll on the mosaics, a remarkable number have survived. Stunning pieces have been uncovered throughout northern Libya, and some of the museums contain a treasure trove of mosaic art. A dream tour for mosaic enthusiasts would take in Qasr Libya (*see p78*) and Tolmeita (*see pp76–7*) museums in Cyrenaica, as well as the museums of Sabratha (*see p57*), Leptis Magna (*see p53*) and Tripoli (*see pp37–41*) in Tripolitania. Sabratha's Seaward Baths and Cyrene's House of Jason Magnus are among the monuments that still feature examples of mosaics in their original settings.

A Roman mosaic at Sabratha

Villa Sileen (see p60), near Leptis, is full of amazing mosaics from the Roman period, although unfortunately it was closed for renovations at the time of writing.

Libya's collections of mosaics cover a fascinating variety of subjects and provide a creative testament to an eclectic mix of influences. There are depictions of gods, mythological and religious iconography, but there are also scenes from everyday life and some portrayals of specific public events. In Villa Sileen there is a mosaic depicting citizens of Leptis enjoying a day at the circus. Sabratha's museum has some excellent mythological mosaics, such as the winged horse Pegasus and the venerated wine god Bacchus. The 'Four Seasons' is one of the most recurrent motifs across Libya's mosaic collection. Impressive works based on this theme, all rendered slightly differently, can be seen in Tolmeita, Villa Sileen, the Jamahiriya Museum and the House of Jason Magnus, among others. There is also a common preoccupation with the natural world; peacocks, lions and fish are some of the diverse creatures depicted in a number of mosaics. The Byzantine mosaic panels of Qasr Libya show a strong cultural link to Egypt, for the Nile appears to have been very influential and two of the panels include images of the famous Lighthouse of Alexandria.

Libya's mosaics also vary in scale and in the level of thematic complication. Some are small, with a lovely simplicity, such as those at Qasr Libya. Others are like vast fragmented tapestries. The floor mosaics in the museums at Sabratha and in Tripoli are examples of how stunning these large-scale works can be.

Jebel al-Akhdar

The countryside of the Jebel al-Akhdar ('Green Mountains') is like nowhere else in Libya. This mountainous, forested region is astonishingly lush in winter and retains its green aspect even through the summer months. It is easy to see why this landscape of cliffs, valleys, caves and wooded areas was at the forefront of the resistance during the Italian occupation. One of the key areas, both historically and scenically, is **Wadi al-Kuf**, a deep valley full of atmospheric caves (*see p124*). Wadi al-Kuf is located to the east of Qasr Libya.

Ras al-Hillal and L'Atrun

The village of Ras al-Hillal ('Head of Crescent') is set on a beautiful crescent bay east of Apollonia. In the 6th century AD, this region was a significant outpost for the Byzantine Coptic Christians and over 50 churches have been discovered in the vicinity, 14 of which have been excavated. The ruins of three such churches can be explored at Ras al-Hillal and neighbouring L'Atrun. The most intact is the Western Church at L'Atrun, where distinctive Coptic crosses can be seen on the marble columns. Despite, or even partly because of ongoing excavations, the

Byzantine church at L'Atrun

church has an atmospheric charm. Pieces of pottery found on the site have been gathered into a little garden, while slabs of marble lie in the baptistery. The mosaic floor has not weathered time very well, but there are a few details of tigers and birds visible alongside geometric patterns. This being farmland, the ruins have sheep and camels among their neighbours.
Open site. Free admission.

Al Bayda

Al Bayda has several decent hotels and restaurants and makes an agreeable base for visiting the nearby sites. Being on high ground, it has a relatively mild climate. There is little to see in the town itself, apart from the 4th-century BC **Temple of Aesculapius**, which is located just west of the town centre. Aesculapius was the god of healing and the temple features carvings of the

Stone carvings at Slonta's temple

now-extinct silphium plant, which was famed for its medicinal properties (*see pp70–71*). Al Bayda also boasts some attractive architecture, most notably the Omar al-Mukhtar University and the Bilal Mosque.

Slonta

The small village of Slonta, near Al Bayda, is the site of an ancient stone temple that pre-dates the arrival of the Greeks and as such has historic significance. Although only a small area of the temple remains, there are numerous clearly visible faces, figures and animals carved into the rock. One of the animals is a large snake, thought to represent a snake-god.

THE HERO OF THE RESISTANCE

During the Italian occupation, the notoriously rebellious Cyrenaica region was the location of the most dramatic fighting and suffering in Libya. Omar al-Mukhtar, a Sanusi sheikh and resistance fighter, united the local tribes and led a long campaign for freedom. His base was the caves of the scenic Wadi al-Kuf (*see p124*). During his life, al-Mukhtar was known as the 'Lion of the Desert', and since his capture and execution in 1931, at the age of 73, he has been revered as a national hero. His picture is on the 10 LD note, the university in Al Bayda bears his name, and there is a film, *Lion of the Desert* (1981), based on his life.

Jebel Nafusa and Ghadames

Travel just a short distance inland from coastal Tripolitania, up into the hills of the Jebel Nafusa ('Western Mountains'), and a completely different side of Libya emerges. This jagged landscape is a stronghold of Berber culture, past and present, marked by fantastical architecture and hilltop villages. Southwest of the Jebel Nafusa is one of Libya's unique gems, the captivating old oasis town of Ghadames.

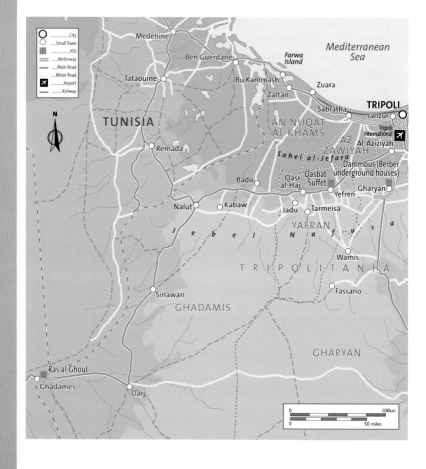

○	City
○	Small Town
■	POI
	Motorway
	Main Road
	Minor Road
✈	Airport
	Railway

N

Medenine

Ben Guerdane

Tataouine

TUNISIA

Remada

Nalut

Kabaw

Badir

Qasr al-Haj

Qasbat Suffet

Jadu

Tarmeisa

J e b e l   N a f u s a

Sinawan

GHADAMIS

Ras al-Ghoul

Ghadames

Darj

Farwa Island

Bu Kammash

Zaltan

Zuara

Sabratha

S a h e l   a l - J e f a r a

AN NUQAT AL KHAMS

AZ ZAWIYAH

Al-Aziziyah

Dammous (Berber underground houses)

Yefren

Gharyan

YAFRAN

Wamis

T R I P O L I T A N I A

Fassano

GHARYAN

Mediterranean Sea

TRIPOLI

Janzur

Tripoli International

0   100km

0   50 miles

A view over the plains of the Jebel Nafusa

The old stone villages and fortified granary stores of the Jebel Nafusa share some characteristics with the old city of Ghadames. One of the uniting factors is the extraordinarily inventive use of mud bricks, stone, gypsum and palm wood in the architecture. Another is the sense of abandonment that clings to all these places. During the second half of the 20th century, government modernisation schemes caused the relocation of entire communities from their traditional homes to new settlements nearby. Although this happened all over the country, it had a particularly dramatic effect on the Jebel Nafusa and Ghadames areas. The old towns here have an ethereal quality and many of the sites evoke science fiction or fantasy film sets, yet they are also monuments to a very practical past. This contrast is exemplified in the Berber fortified granaries of the Jebel Nafusa. These fascinating structures are called *qasrs* (castles), but their primary use was as storage rooms for grain and other supplies. Ghadames is aesthetically stunning, but it also represents a triumph of engineering over the harsh desert climate. In its heyday, this town in the middle of nowhere was an important and sophisticated centre for the caravan trade across the Sahara.

The landscape of the Jebel Nafusa and that of the desert plain leading to Ghadames is also distinctive. Striking red and yellow ochre runs through the rock of the mountainsides, while the sand across part of the desert plain is an orange-red colour. In other places the land is surprisingly green, with lots of trees and grasses that make it almost resemble a savannah.

Ghadames

Despite its isolated position, the oasis town of Ghadames has an eventful history. This unique corner of Libya has seen occupations, fierce battles and a lucrative caravan trade. Mystery shrouds the area's early history, but it is known that the Romans occupied the site for over two centuries from 19 BC and named the town Cydamus. Later, in the 6th century AD, Ghadames was occupied by the Byzantines and then further influenced by the arrival of Greek missionaries. In AD 668 the character of the town was changed again, definitively this time, when it was conquered by the Islamic armies and the Berber inhabitants converted to another new religion. After several different towns had been built on the site, the old city you see today was constructed around the early 13th century. Between the 13th and 19th centuries, notwithstanding the odd struggle with the powers that be, Ghadames enjoyed a good degree of autonomy and flourished as a caravan trade centre. Trouble arrived in the 19th and 20th centuries. Economically weakened following the decline of Saharan trade and occupied for years by first the Ottomans and then the Italians, Ghadames was hit hard during World War II. In a misguided attack against the Italians, Allied forces bombed the city, killing 40 people and damaging hundreds of buildings.

The old city of Ghadames continued to be inhabited until the 1980s, when the Libyan government built a new town outside the city walls and gave a new house to each family. Enticed by modern conveniences such as running water and by the fact that they were able to keep their old houses as well, everyone eventually moved out. Luckily, the outside world began to recognise that Ghadames was special. In 1986, the old city was designated a UNESCO World Heritage Site, and the United Nations Development Programme became involved in restoration work in

A quiet path in Ghadames

Traditional embroidered slippers are made in Ghadames

1999. Many of the families who moved out still maintain their original houses and some open them to visitors. Today, as a result of these efforts and helped by income from tourism, the old city is in a good state of preservation.

The new town has little to interest visitors, especially when compared with the charm of the old city, but it makes a pleasant base. An elegant new mosque beautifies the cityscape, although non-Muslims are not permitted inside. Ghadames has a good choice of hotels, a few restaurants (often closed in summer, which is the low season) and a small number of interesting souvenir shops. Look out for the traditional shoe shop near the museum, a family business producing distinctive embroidered boots and slippers. There is also an Internet café, a post office and a laundry. Ghadames is known as one of the most conservative parts of Libya, which you may observe in the dress of the local women.

Museum
The building that is now home to the Ghadames museum dates from the Italian era, when it was a police station. It is a low-lying building set around a landscaped courtyard, which you cross to move between the different rooms. Room 1 is the most interesting as it is concerned with the history of the old city. The exhibits include old

photographs, information about the trans-Saharan trade routes that were so significant in Ghadames, and examples of the renowned embroidered shoes. A small annexe holds glass cabinets full of herbal remedies, labelled to say what they were used for. Room 2 showcases the Roman ruins found in the town, while room 3 has a Tuareg theme, with objects such as camel seats and a tent. Finally, room 4, which is next to the small shop, is mostly about architecture. It has maps, plans and samples of building materials, including gypsum in different stages of refinement. There is also an interesting display of desert roses (fossilised sand) in this room. The museum has toilets, which is worth noting as you will not find any public toilets inside the old city.

Open: 9am–1.30pm. Admission & camera/video charges.

Old city

Exploring the old city is an unforgettable experience. This is a place of contrasts, a well-ordered maze of covered streets where the interplay of light and shadow is almost an architectural feature. There were two main tribes in old Ghadames: the Bani Walid and the Bani Wazid. They occupied half of the city each and were subdivided into seven smaller tribes between them, with each of these groups taking a section or 'street' of the city. Consequently, the old city has seven entrances and seven main streets. This sense of order extended into all aspects of the design and community of the city. The buildings, some 1,600 of them in total, including 1,250 houses and 21 mosques, are squeezed compactly into the centre. Between the buildings and the city walls, gardens

A palm garden in Ghadames

89

Jebel Nafusa and Ghadames

full of palm trees fan out, creating a green belt which has an almost tropical feel. Back in the covered area, stone benches line the walls. As well as being good seats on which to relax and keep cool, the benches served as meeting places whenever there was something to be discussed as a community. When issues of city-wide importance arose, the eldest men from each community formed a council in the central square to reach a decision.

One of Ghadames' 21 mosques

USES OF THE PALM TREE

The palm tree has always taken centre stage among the flora of Libya, but in old Ghadames this extraordinarily versatile plant was especially significant. All parts of the tree had a useful role to play in the construction and life of the city. The sturdy trunk made great doors and roofs, while the thinner branches and fronds were fashioned into chairs and tables. Fires were lit with the cereals, and ropes were twisted out of the fibrous tissue. Twenty-five different types of dates grew in the area and those of low quality made nutritious food for the goats.

The main square was very significant in a number of ways. It was a meeting point for the two halves of the city and also a centre for caravans to pass through. The two oldest mosques in the city are located here, one for each of the main tribes. The **Atik Mosque** (Bani Walid), labelled with a plaque saying 'old mosque', sadly sustained terrible damage in the World War II bombing, but the **Yunis Mosque** (Bani Wazid) is one of five old city mosques still in use today. Near the Atik Mosque, a sign on the wall marks the spot of the 'old post office', which was essentially a hanging basket where people deposited their letters. Another important feature of the square is *al-kadus*, the place of time and water management (*see pp90–91*). You need a guide to explore the old city. Mahmud Al Asuad, who was born in the old city, merits a mention and there are many other local guides who know the old city very well.

Admission & camera/video charges.

Ghadames

In the golden era of the old city, Ghadames was one of the most significant hubs on the Saharan trade routes. Aside from the famous embroidered slippers, Ghadames was not a centre of production. Instead, it provided a convenient setting for a thriving market. Goods brought by traders from the south included precious metals and stones, and animal products such as ivory and ostrich feathers. Products from the north included cotton, linen, manufactured goods, Parisian pearls and Venetian glass necklaces. The traders all converged on the main square in Ghadames, where they contributed greatly to the energy and drive of the town. The caravans also brought letters, news and returning travellers, keeping Ghadames in touch with the outside world.

Another reason for the town's importance on the caravan routes was its water supply. Libyan societies have always been concerned with how best to conserve and manage water supplies, and the system developed in the old city of Ghadames was one of the most inventive. Underground canals, which can still be seen today, supplied water from the main well to the buildings and gardens, but this was not automatic. Guardians were appointed to sit in the main square measuring out the water. The water flowed from the source into a large bottle holding about 4 litres (1 gallon). The guardian's job was to empty it slowly through a small hole into the canal, which took about three minutes. He kept track of these

A covered alleyway in Ghadames

units by tying knots in a palm leaf, thereby recording both how much water had been used and what time of day it was. The bottle and the niche where the guardian sat were both called *al-kadus*, while the unit of time and water was referred to as one *kadus*. *Al-kadus* was one element of the culture of organisation which extended to all the routines of everyday life in the city.

The traditional houses of Ghadames are the city's most vivid feature. These closely packed homes were all designed following the same model. They typically had four levels, linked by narrow staircases. There would be an entrance room on the ground floor, the main living area on the first floor, bedrooms and storage on the first and second floors, and a kitchen on the roof. The houses were essentially feminine, in contrast to the masculine streets. While the men of the town converged in organised groups out in the lanes and squares, the women lived their lives inside their homes or up on the rooftops. As the houses were so close together, women could cross the roofs to visit each other. They also held their own public ceremonies and a weekly market on the rooftops. Women were responsible for the elaborate, colourful interiors that give the houses their decorative impact. The houses feel warm and lived in, but

Inside a traditional house

they could also be places of solemnity. While men attended public funerals, women would observe their mourning rituals indoors. On their wedding night, a newly married couple would retreat into a small arched canopy room off the living room. This was only ever used once more at the most: if a woman was widowed, she would spend over four months confined to this room before being free to remarry.

Qasr al-Haj

The *qasr* (castle or fortified granary) in the village of Qasr al-Haj is spectacular. Unlike the other *qasrs* in the region, this one has a circular structure, with the cave-like storage rooms arranged around an enclosed courtyard. Also unusual is that some of the rooms are still used for storage by local families. The *qasr* was built more than 800 years ago in order to store harvests of barley and wheat. Some of these grains were donated to pilgrims on their way to Mecca and, in keeping with the religious theme, the *qasr* has 114 rooms, the same as the number of verses in the Quran.

Just inside the heavy palm door, there is an entrance passage with a mini-museum of traditional Berber household items laid out in stone alcoves. This collection includes everything from shoes and cooking utensils to an eyeliner applicator. The passageway leads straight into the courtyard, from where you can peek into the storage rooms at ground level and climb a set of stone steps to explore the upper level. A ledge runs all the way around the circumference. It is generally quite wide, but the width varies in places and care should be taken as there is no barrier at the edge. The steps should also be climbed with caution as they are narrow and fairly uneven. The caretaker opens the *qasr* whenever there are visitors. Outside the *qasr* there is a decent public toilet.
Admission charge.

Nalut

The town of Nalut has modern amenities such as a hotel, restaurant and shops, alongside an old settlement and fascinating *qasr*. Nalut is situated at a high point of the Jebel Nafusa, 760m (2,500ft) above sea level, and enjoys a great view over the surrounding landscape. The roads from Tripoli and Ghadames meet at a roundabout in the centre of Nalut. As you arrive in the town centre, you will be sure to notice a prominent dinosaur statue. This curiosity marks the spot where a dinosaur skeleton was discovered in the 1990s. There is a festival in Nalut, 10–12 April every year (*see p18*).

Olive-oil presses

There are two old stone olive-oil presses in Nalut. One is just to the side of the path between the car park and the *qasr*, while the other is a little further away, off the path which leads west from the *qasr*. The *qasr* caretaker (*see below*) has a key and can show you the way. The presses form a fascinating addition to the *qasr*. Using the same philosophy of keeping produce cool, they were built in cellar-like rooms carved into the rock of the mountain. Inside, each cellar is dominated by a large circular stone slab that was used to grind the olives. The resourceful inhabitants harnessed camel power to turn the stone. There is just enough space for a camel to walk in circles around it. Further back in the room is a heavy beam attached to a rope pulley system,

An old olive press at Qasr Nalut

which was used to further crush the olives, and storage spaces where the oil was kept.

Qasr

Nalut's *qasr* is another curiosity. It has no central courtyard. Instead, the storage rooms are stacked up on either side of two narrow twisting alleyways in an arrangement that appears labyrinthine and almost haphazard. It evokes the kind of village you might expect to see in a science fiction film. The *qasr* covers an area of 1,700sq m (2,000sq yds) and has 400 storage rooms. It was constructed in the 13th century over the ruins of a much older building. The *qasr* is looked after by caretaker Khalid Boswa, who is also a local artist. He displays his carved limestone souvenirs for sale just outside. *Open: daylight hours & possibly later on request. Tel: (caretaker) 092 425 3526. Admission charge.*

The courtyard at Kabaw's *qasr,* featuring palm trunk doors

Kabaw

Along with Nalut and Qasr al-Haj, Kabaw completes a trilogy of enchanting Berber *qasrs*. The fortified granary in this sleepy hilltop town is different again from the examples at Nalut and Qasr al-Haj, mainly because it is smaller and the rooms are arranged in a patchwork effect. In fact, the *qasr* here was built in stages and was a joint effort between many contributors. A central courtyard was established and then layers of rooms, 360 in total, were gradually added to the structure. The granary became the centre of the community and people who had originally lived in scattered villages in the mountains gradually gravitated towards it. Each family had a room or two, depending on the size of the family, and these were passed down through the generations. Sadly, the *qasr* was badly damaged during heavy rains in the winter of 1975–6 and has not been used for storage since. The traditional underground stone houses of the old town of Kabaw were ruined in the same rains and similarly abandoned. What remains of the old town can be seen outside the granary walls.

In 1990, the local people decided to restore the *qasr* and celebrate their heritage with a carnival. The *qasr* festival (*see p18*) is not consistently annual and there is no set timetable for which years it will take place, but if you are planning a trip to the area in April, it is worth finding out if the festival will be happening. It is a great way to experience Berber culture and folklore. Kabaw also has a number of old olive presses, like the ones at Nalut.

Ras al-Ghoul

Ras al-Ghoul ('Mountain of Ghosts') is an ancient desert castle, just 10km (6 miles) from Ghadames but with an isolated aspect. Built on a strange small rocky hill in the middle of flat desert, the castle was the site of a famous siege in AD 668, when some of the residents of Ghadames fled there in defiance of the Islamic soldiers who were conquering the country.

Today, the main attraction of Ras al-Ghoul is its unique vantage point across chains of sand dunes that lie in three countries; Ras al-Ghoul is just a short distance from both the Algerian and Tunisian borders. The view is often enhanced by spectacular sunsets, and late afternoon trips from Ghadames are popular. You can watch the sun set from the castle itself or climb a nearby dune for a higher panorama. During high season, there is usually a Tuareg camp here. Take care when climbing to the castle as there is a shaft just at the top of the path.

The sun goes down at Ras al-Ghoul

Berber architecture

The mountainous Jebel Nafusa region has been a sanctuary of Berber culture in Libya since the Arab invasion of the 7th century. Historians have been unable to reach a consensus over whether the Berbers are descended from the original Neolithic inhabitants of the area or from the Garamantians of further south. Either way, the tribes now known collectively as Berbers definitely pre-dated the arrival of the Arab tribes. In Roman times, the indigenous people of the North African coast were described as *barbari*, and it is thought that the name 'Berber' was derived from this word. The term is now used to define a number of communities who are united by a distinctive culture and by the fact that they speak native dialects, usually in addition to Arabic.

The *qasr* at Kabaw

The Berbers who took refuge in the Jebel Nafusa hundreds of years ago set about constructing extraordinary but practical structures, from concealed underground houses to fortress-like granaries. In this barren landscape, preserving food was essential, which explains the effort put into the construction of the fortified granary stores. The granaries are called *qasrs* (castles) and their impressive appearance certainly merits this name. They were mostly built in the 12th century, using a sturdy mix of stones, clay and mud, with gypsum as a sealant and palm trunks for doors. Each of the *qasrs* has a unique design in terms of how the storage rooms are arranged, but they all have more than one level. Dried produce such as barley and wheat was kept in the rooms above ground, while olive oil was typically stored in the cooler rooms below ground, where it could be preserved for up to about six years.

The inhabitants of each village lived in a community-minded way, ensuring that there would always be enough food for all by making stockpiling obligatory. The founder of the *qasr* at Qasr al-Haj, a man named Sheikh Abu Jatla, even developed a tax system. He charged a rent in barley or wheat for

Qasr al-Haj – the main courtyard of the fortified granary

use of the rooms and distributed these gains to passing pilgrims or the poor. He also sold some of the produce to finance a mosque and Quranic teachers. At Kabaw, small quantities of the dates, figs, flour and olive oil stored in the rooms were given as a salary to the *qasr* guardian. All the *qasrs* were vital hubs for the tight-knit communities they served, and some had specific social functions. In Kabaw, a public meeting was called in the courtyard of the *qasr* whenever there was something to be discussed, and if somebody had lost something, they could make use of a 'lost and found' system there. Meanwhile, Nalut's

qasr doubled as an open-air town hall. *Qasrs* were also often employed as marketplaces or rest-stops for pilgrims.

The intriguing underground houses of the Jebel Nafusa functioned on the same principles of needing protection from the elements and from potential invaders. Like the *qasrs*, these *dammous* fit harmoniously with the rocky landscape and demonstrate ingenious use of natural materials. They are also known as 'troglodyte' houses, an evocative term that summons up images of self-sufficient communities sealing themselves off from the outside world, safe as hidden houses.

Gharyan area

The town of Gharyan is not very interesting in itself, but it has two main attractions: underground Berber houses and a huge pottery market. On the practical front, Gharyan is useful for providing a couple of hotels, places to grab a bite to eat, a post office and Internet café. All are located around Sharia al-Jamahiriya in the town centre.

Dammous
(Berber underground houses)

The underground (or troglodyte) houses in the Gharyan area provide an insight into the practical traditions of the ancient Berber people. These stone warren-like dwellings were the perfect solution to staying cool in summer, warm in winter and safe at all times. None of the houses are inhabited now, their owners having moved with the times into modern houses above ground, but some are open to visitors. A good example is Belhaj Troglodyte, just outside Gharyan, which is run by the family who used to live in it (and who now maintain it from a villa next door). The house is set around a 'courtyard', effectively a round pit, which is the only thing visible from ground level. On all sides of the

Troglodyte house, Gharyan

courtyard there are surprisingly spacious rooms cut into the rock. Your tour guide can arrange a visit, and for large groups (about ten plus), the family can provide a traditional lunch or dinner in the house. Thanks to the installation of a bathroom, it is even possible to complete the experience by spending a night here.

Pottery market

The Jebel Nafusa area is known for its pottery, and no town demonstrates this more thoroughly than Gharyan, which is effectively the pottery capital of Libya. The town is home to a huge roadside market devoted exclusively to pottery. Colourful ceramic wares spill out of a chain of stalls along the road into Gharyan from Tripoli. Just south of Sharia al-Jamahiriya there is a crafts school open to visitors, where artisans demonstrate traditional rug-weaving as well as pottery-making. Your tour guide should be able to arrange a visit. The nearby village of Bughilan is also a pottery centre, and you may see small stalls in other spots as well.

Tarmeisa

The ancient Berber village of Tarmeisa (or Tormisa) sits at one of the highest points of the Jebel Nafusa and hence boasts a panoramic view. Tarmeisa was abandoned in the 1950s and is now a ghost village of empty stone houses, doorways and tunnels, made all the more atmospheric by their cliff-edge setting. The village used to be closed up each

Wares on display at the pottery market in Gharyan

night by the raising of a drawbridge, which was the only means of access over a cavernous drop at the entrance. Now long gone, the drawbridge has been replaced by a bridged road at the approach to the car park.
Open site. Free admission.

Yefren

Like Tarmeisa, the town of Yefren is advantageously situated high up in the mountains and there are great views from here. Yefren has ruins of an old town and an even older synagogue. There is also a Roman mausoleum, called Qasbat Suffet, outside the town. If you need directions to the sights, ask at the only hotel in Yefren (*see p171*), which also has a particularly stunning vista from its terrace.

Drive: Sabratha and the Jebel Nafusa

This driving tour of the Jebel Nafusa takes in the ancient coastal city of Sabratha, as well as a number of distinctive locations in the mountainous Jebel Nafusa. Expect panoramic views and incredible architecture, including traditional Berber qasrs *(fortified granaries) and an underground house.*

Allow two full days for the 700km (435-mile) tour, plus an optional second night at the troglodyte house in Gharyan.

Starting in Tripoli, take the main coastal road west to Sabratha, 69km (43 miles) from the capital. Set off early to give you a few hours in Sabratha before the drive into the Jebel Nafusa.

1 Sabratha

Sabratha's must-see monument is its spectacular theatre, but this beautiful Punic-Roman site also boasts one of Libya's best museums and a great seafront location (*see pp56–60*).
Return to the main road and head back towards Tripoli. Turn off at Surman and take the road south. After around 80km (50 miles), you will reach a main junction. Turn right, toward Nalut. After a few kilometres, when you get to a little village, follow the road round to the right. After about 30km (18¹/₂ miles), turn left off the road to reach Qasr al-Haj.

2 Qasr al-Haj

The enclosed circular *qasr* here is a great introduction to the fortified granaries of the region (*see p92*).

Continue west along the same road to Nalut, approximately 150km (93 miles).

3 Nalut

Nalut is an atmospheric place to spend the night. The view at sunset can be incredible and the *qasr* is illuminated after dark. In the morning, explore the *qasr* and olive presses (*see p92*).
Continue southwest out of Nalut for a few kilometres, then take a left turn. Take another left at the first main junction. After 25km (15 miles), look out for a left turn. Kabaw is about 9km (5¹/₂ miles) north of the main road.

4 Kabaw

Kabaw has a distinctive *qasr* and a restaurant (*see p172*) where you can pause for lunch.
Go back to the main road and turn left. Follow the road east to Tarmeisa, about 80km (50 miles). You will pass the town of Jadu shortly before reaching the turn-off for Tarmeisa.

5 Tarmeisa

Stop in the car park just across the bridge into the village and walk to the cliff-edge to see the ruins of the old town and the panoramic view (*see p99*).

Go back over the bridge and continue east along the main road. After you pass through the town of Zintan, it is about 30km (18½ miles) to Yefren, which is a left turn-off.

6 Yefren

Yefren is another scenically located mountain town, with some interesting historical architecture (*see p99*).

Continue east from Yefren to Gharyan, approximately 70km (43 miles).

7 Gharyan pottery

You cannot miss the pottery market that lines the side of the main road. *There is a dammous (troglodyte house) just outside Gharyan, a short way south of the Rabta Hotel in the centre of town. It is signposted from the main road by a yellow sign reading 'troglodyte'.*

8 Troglodyte house

If you are part of a group, you may be able to arrange dinner and accommodation in the troglodyte house (ask your tour company). If not, at least explore and pause for a mint tea.

Return to the main road and go north to Tripoli, a journey of roughly 85km (53 miles).

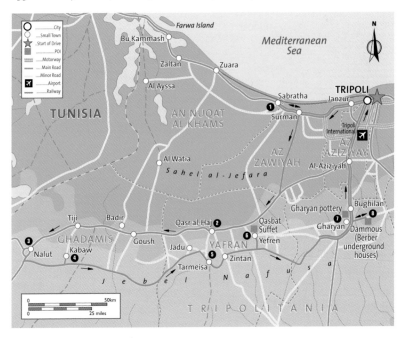

Fezzan and Sahara

In Libya the desert looms large, not just physically but also in the cultural and historical fabric of the country. The Sahara, one of the most inhospitable environments on Earth, is surprisingly accessible in Libya. It is also an amazingly diverse landscape, encompassing every possible arrangement of sand and rock, from golden dunes to craggy cliffs. Remarkable prehistoric rock art and opportunities to glimpse a traditional desert way of life complete the experience.

The highlights of this vast region include amazing sand dunes and ethereal rock formations sheltering paintings which date back thousands of years. The history of the Fezzan region, which encompasses most of the Libyan Sahara, was shaped differently from that of northern Libya. There are no ruins of ancient European civilisations here. Instead, the local Garamantians ruled supreme in ancient times, managing to build an empire in this

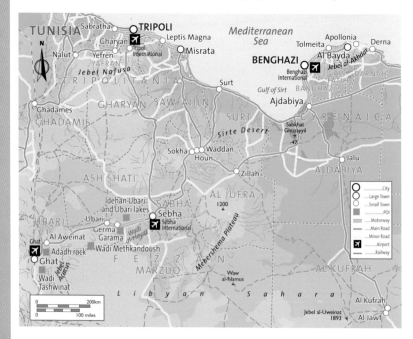

Stunning scenery in Jebel Acacus

harshest of lands. Throughout the centuries, trans-Saharan caravan trade routes connected the Libyan Sahara to the rest of Africa and to the coast.

Nowadays, although the majority of Libyans live in the cities of the north, the desert is sparsely populated with small but culturally significant communities. Most notable are the Tuareg (*see pp16–17*), a traditionally nomadic people. Although many Tuareg have settled near the cities in recent years, some still choose a rural desert lifestyle. Some Tuareg have developed a new trade of selling jewellery and crafts to tourists, which means visitors have a good chance of meeting these fascinating people.

Jebel Acacus

The Jebel Acacus is a UNESCO World Heritage Site and one of the most spellbinding places in Libya. Phenomenally shaped rocks rise out of the sand as steep walls, ridges, natural arches and bizarre stand-alone structures. This ethereal landscape features great panoramic views if you are up to some short climbs. The main attractions of the area are the abundant ancient rock paintings and carvings that decorate many of the rock faces. They are complemented by natural features, such as beautiful seams of purple, yellow, red and blue running through the stone. The paintings are a testament to the region's history, a lasting record of the animals who once roamed the Sahara and the lifestyle of the people who once called it home. The Acacus is a heartland of the Tuareg, and a few families still live a nomadic lifestyle here. Others have moved on but sometimes return to show visitors around. Navigating around the Jebel Acacus is a complicated task, so travelling with a guide is highly recommended. It is difficult to find detailed maps, but

A natural rock arch in the Acacus

Jebel Acacus: Tourist Map and Guide by EWP (*www.ewpnet.com*) is a noteworthy exception.

Awiss

In the northern Awiss region stands one of the most fantastic single rocks of the Acacus: the **Adadh rock**. This towering example of a natural sculpture is almost 20m (65ft) high and is known as 'finger rock' or 'thumb rock' because of its distinctive shape. There is a wealth of rock art sites to the south of Adadh, particularly concentrated around Wadi Tiheden. They include paintings and engravings of animals and human figures, some of which contain a striking level of detail. The area also boasts some of the best views in the Acacus.

Southern Acacus

This area used to be easily reached from the oasis town of Ghat, but at the time of writing, the road south of Ghat was closed due to a border dispute between Libya and Algeria. If the road reopens, there is a gateway to the Acacus from the south side. If not, this region can only be accessed by driving all the way through off-road. This remote area is the location of more amazing rock art sites. Highlights include carvings of elephants, giraffes and camels and large paintings of women. The south also boasts great panoramic views and the tallest natural arch in the Acacus: the Afozedzhar Arch.

The Adadh rock is known as 'thumb rock'

Wadi Tashwinat

The Wadi Tashwinat area at the centre of the Acacus is home to a high concentration of stunning rock paintings. It is a vast maze-like landscape with a wild beauty about it. Wadi Tashwinat is huge, almost 60km (37 miles) long, and the main valley, criss-crossed with a series of tributary valleys, is effectively a gallery of rock art. There are sites scattered throughout, mainly in sheltered spots such as caves, ledges and under overhanging sections of rock. Many of the sites are marked by yellow Department of Antiquities signs and protected behind palm fences, but some are unmarked. Among the many highlights are painted scenes providing a glimpse into the lives of the people who once lived in this valley, including a beautiful wedding scene and a dramatic hunting scene. Although paintings make up most of the art here, there are also some fantastic engravings. A well called Aminaner marks the entrance to Wadi Tashwinat from the Awiss area. Aminaner (co-ordinates N 24°51′ 34.21″ E 10°39′ 38.59″) is a good source of water for washing, but tourists should avoid drinking from it.

Saharan rock art

The rock paintings and carvings of the Sahara were effectively hidden treasures until relatively recently, known only to the inhabitants of the area and the odd European explorer. This all changed in the 1950s, when Professor Fabrizio Mori and a team from the University of Rome arrived in the Jebel Acacus to study the rock art and bring it to the notice of the outside world for the first time. Their work was furthered in the 1990s by another Italian expedition. The archaeological teams documented an abundance of sites where rock faces are decorated with paintings and engravings of human figures, wild beasts, domesticated animals and symbols. These extraordinary images, deep in the heart of the Sahara, have provided significant insight into the physical and cultural history of the area.

Rock paintings, Wadi Tiheden

Libya's rock art can be broadly categorised according to historical periods, with different eras producing distinct styles and themes. Precise dating is often not possible, but it is thought that the oldest engravings may be as much as 12,000 years old. Between 10,000 and 6000 BC, the Sahara was a fertile savannah. The earliest rock art hails from this period, generally described as the 'Wild Fauna Period' because of the predominance of large wild animals such as elephants, giraffes and a species of giant buffalo (now long extinct). The later part of this era (8000 to 6000 BC) overlapped with the development of a new style known as the 'Round Head Period'. This marked the appearance of human figures, usually of simplistic, featureless form, with characteristic round heads.

From 5500 to 2000 BC was the 'Pastoral Period'. The climate of the Sahara was becoming drier and it is thought that the early nomadic communities were becoming more settled. The rock paintings they produced featured people in celebratory or pastoral scenes. Images of domestic cattle and hunters with weapons date from this time. Cattle

Rock carving of giraffes at Wadi Tashwinat

also featured in the next period, the 'Horse Period' (from 1000 BC), along with, predictably, horses. Fascinating images of horse-drawn chariots show how transport was developing. The human figures of this later era are intriguingly stylised, with two triangles for bodies topped by circular heads. Finally, there was the 'Camel Period' (from 200 BC), starring, unsurprisingly, camels, which have become icons of the desert. The more recent rock paintings and engravings, which also include inscriptions in the Tuareg script, are less figurative and considered less skilfully executed than early works. Interestingly, artists often painted over or next to earlier examples, creating a layered effect resulting in some rock faces being literally covered in images.

Many of the carvings in the Libyan Sahara are huge. These giant figures of animals and sometimes humans almost seem to stride across the rock faces or peer down from on high. The paintings, conversely, are often small and minutely detailed. They have a natural colour palette of ochre, white and red, which amazingly still stands out clearly from the rock. Sadly, some of the paintings have been damaged by tourists in the past trying to make copies or even chip away parts of the rock. The government's decision to enforce guided tourism was greatly influenced by these careless actions. The **Trust for African Rock Art**, based in Kenya, is a source of information about the protection of rock art across the Sahara (*www.africanrockart.org*).

Drive: Jebel Acacus

Touring the open-air gallery of the Jebel Acacus is an incredible Saharan experience. The two mini-tours suggested here feature some of the most interesting rock art sites in the area. Bear in mind that the Acacus, like much of the Sahara, poses a navigational challenge. These descriptions are intended to give you some idea of where sites are located, but travelling with an experienced guide is essential.

Ideally, allow two days to explore all these sites, one full day for each tour.

Tour 1: Wadi Tashwinat
Begin by driving to the southern end of the valley and work your way back northeast.

1 Wan Melol/Uan Amil
(N 24°50′ 25.89″ E 10°30′ 09.35″)
This site is designated as 'Wan Melol' on a yellow Department of Antiquities sign, but named as 'Uan Amil' on a sign by the Italian-Libyan Archaeological Mission. The paintings here include a wedding scene. The level of detail is astonishing.

2 Wan Muhuggiag and natural arch
(N 24°51′ 24.45″ E 10°34′ 41.12″)
One of the area's incredible natural rock arches is located here, along with some varied paintings.

3 Takdhalt
(N 24°51′ 07.58″ E 10°31′ 09.16″)
Under a jutting ridge, behind the yellow sign naming the site as 'Takdhalt', is a collection of paintings including human figures and Tuareg Tifinagh letters. There is also a map carved into the rock, although this has weathered.

4 Elephants
(N 24°51′ 36.69″ E 10°32′ 16.95″)
These two carved elephants are thought to be among the oldest works in the Acacus. The larger is in a fantastic state of preservation, while the smaller is more faded but still visible.

5 Wan Traghit
(N 24°51′ 21.52″ E 10°32′ 25.09″)
Just east of the elephants is this site featuring some of the region's most amazing paintings, including a vivid hunting scene. The delicate rendering of the painting contrasts with the subject matter: a hunter and his prey.

Tour 2: Awiss
The Awiss region is almost due north from the main sites of Wadi Tashwinat.

1 Wadi Tiheden
(N 25°16′ 01.25″ E 10°35′ 45.13″)
Here you will see some skilfully rendered fighting scenes. The weapons and helmets are wonderfully detailed.

2 Wadi Udhohen
(N 25°17′ 12.88″ E 10°34′ 53.12″)
This site includes an excellent chariot painting.

3 East of Tihe-n-Awiss
(N 25°20′ 00.49″ E 10°31′ 19.52″)

There is a variety of paintings and carvings around this area, a little northwest of Wadi Tiheden. They include a range of animals and human figures from different periods.

4 Adadh
(N 25°31′ 18.77″ E 10°35′ 58.70″)
Finally, stop to take a look at the bizarre 'finger rock' (*see p104*). There are also some fantastic panoramic views from the rocky vantage points in this area.

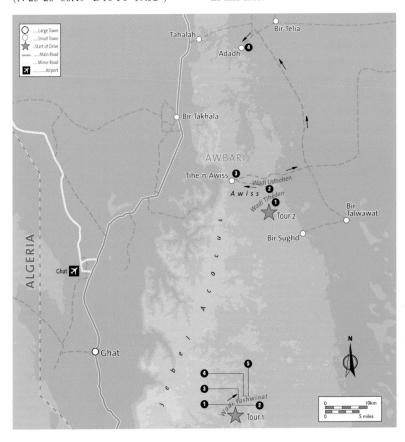

Idehan Ubari and Ubari lakes

For sheer Saharan beauty, the dunes and lakes of the Ubari area are hard to beat. *Idehan* means 'sand-sea', a fitting label for the wave-shaped dunes. It is also sometimes described as an *erg*, which means 'vein'. This is a golden landscape sprinkled with a surprising amount of green. Flat stretches of sand, salt grasses and acacia trees give way to sweeping dunes, which in turn suddenly reveal a flash of green and blue lake. Many of the lakes are now dry, but clumps of palm trees remain where they once were. Gebraoun, Umm al-Maa and Mavo (the three lakes described below) have water and are some of the most picturesque. Unsurprisingly, you have to go off-road to reach the lakes. The main gateway to the lakes is the village of Tekerkiba. Ubari town, situated further west along the main road, is really only worth stopping at if you need practical supplies.

Gebraoun

Gebraoun is the biggest of the Ubari lakes. There are two camps here, offering shady seating, drinks, basic meals and Tuareg crafts for sale. The bigger of the camps, Winzrik, also has a kitchen and palm-roofed dining area for groups, and is adorned with colourful signs in French about the importance of tourism and a unified Africa. For the adventurous, there are also skis and a snowboard for hire. The track leading to Gebraoun lake passes through an abandoned village.

Mavo

Mavo is the lake closest to the Tekerkiba gateway and likely to be the first you see. Although it lacks the atmosphere of Gebraoun and is not quite as beautiful as Umm al-Maa, Mavo is nonetheless an attractive oasis, fringed by palm trees and reeds against a backdrop of sand dunes. Tuareg traders set up silver jewellery stalls overlooking the lake, which must be one of the most singular market locations anywhere.

Umm al-Maa

Umm al-Maa (Mother of Water) is an idyllic representation of oasis scenery. Smaller and prettier than the others, and encircled by palm trees reflected in the water, Umm al-Maa is a good spot for a secluded dip (*see pp120–21*).

Sand dunes in the Ubari area

Gebraoun lake at dawn

Ghat

The ancient oasis town of Ghat was founded by the Garamantes in the 1st century BC on the site of an even older settlement, although the name was not established until much later. Ghat was ruled by the Tuareg, independently of the rest of Libya, for centuries and it remains an important centre for the Tuareg today. The main point of interest is the medina, but Ghat also has a lively weekly market (on Tuesdays) and an annual cultural festival in late December (*see p19*).

Medina

Like the old centres of other towns throughout Libya, Ghat's medina was deserted during the latter part of the last century as the inhabitants moved into new housing. Small but fascinating, the medina showcases typical Saharan building styles. It was constructed of mud bricks, clay, animal dung, straw and palm trunks. As well as the houses that make up most of the medina, there are some public buildings, including a mosque and a sort of town hall. The latter is tall enough to offer great views from its roof. There is also an ancient well. The entrance to the medina is just off the main road through the new town, opposite the town hall. Tickets are purchased from the seller, who will find you as you wander around.
Open: daylight hours. Admission & camera/video charges.

Wadi Methkandoush

Wadi Methkandoush, which stretches southwest of Germa, is another outdoor gallery of prehistoric rock art. Animal carvings are the stars of the show and include stunning portrayals of giraffes, elephants and ostriches. One of the most extraordinary carvings is of two unspecific creatures battling one another on their hind legs. It is possible to visit here on a long day excursion from Germa.

Wan Caza and Idehan Murzuq

Wan Caza is a line of sand dunes rising out of the valley between the Jebel Acacus to the west and the vast Idehan Murzuq (Murzuq sand-sea) to the east. The gently undulating dunes of Wan Caza are like a practice run for the epic sand mountains of nearby Idehan Murzuq, which covers an

THE GARAMANTIANS

The indigenous Garamantian (or Garamantes) people established an empire in southern Libya around 900 BC. While the Mediterranean coast was being colonised by foreign settlers, the Garamantians kept control of the south. Experts at domesticating the desert, they bred horses and herded cattle. From their cultivated city base Garama, they cashed in on the trade opportunities provided by the ancient Saharan caravan routes. They built underground channels to tap the water reserves beneath the sands, enabling them to farm in the middle of the desert. However, this extraordinary solution was not permanent, and by AD 500 the water had run out and the empire declined.

incredible area of over 35,000sq km (13,500sq miles).

Germa

Modern Germa may not be one of Libya's most interesting towns, but it

Dunes at Wan Caza

Desert scene near Germa

has a significant history as the cradle of the Garamantian Empire. In addition to the sites listed here, Germa makes a good base or stopping-off point for visits to nearby areas.

Garama

Garama is a completely different ancient site from those in northern Libya. It was the capital of the Garamantian people from the 1st century AD. Their original settlement was at nearby Zinchecra, of which very little remains. Garama's buildings were sturdily built of stone, clay and dung. Those that have stood the test of time, or been reconstructed to some extent, include a merchant's house, a mosque dating from the Islamic takeover of the town, and some older structures thought to have been a temple and a palace.

Open: May–Sept 8am–7pm; Oct–Apr 9am–5pm. Admission & camera/ video charges.

Museum

Germa's museum offers a good introduction to the geological and archaeological history of the area. Informative photos, maps and charts are displayed on the walls. Among them is a chart showing the different ages of the local rock art. Garamantian artefacts include tombs, objects and jewellery. Of particular note is an ancient mummy that was found in the local area. Some of the explanations are written in English as well as Arabic.

Open: Tue–Sun 8.30am–2pm & 3–6.30pm. Admission & camera/ video charges.

Tombs

In the time of the Garamantes, the areas around ancient Garama and Zinchecra were speckled with burial tombs. The tombs were distinctive, shaped like mini-pyramids with flat tops. Some contained inscriptions or offerings such as pottery, gold or ostrich eggs. Although there are some tombs along the side of the main road between Germa and Ubari, the best place to see them is the Ahramat al-Hattia site. It is located off the main road about 13km (8 miles) west of Germa.

Open: Sat–Thur 9.30am–1.30pm, Fri 3–5pm. Admission & camera/video charges.

A 4WD car is essential in parts of this region

Sebha

Sebha, the largest town of the Libyan Sahara, has little of interest beyond practicalities, but it is extremely useful as most travellers headed into the desert are likely to pass through here. There is an airport with regular flights to Tripoli, a post office, Internet cafés, some decent hotels and worthy restaurants. An Italian fort overlooks the town, but its current military function means no visitors or photographs are permitted. The section of road between Sebha and Germa passes through a surprisingly green valley. This is Wadi al-Hayat ('Valley of Life'), one of the few places in the desert where agriculture can be sustained.

Wadi Meggedet and Kaf Ajnoun

Wadi Meggedet is a collection of valleys hidden behind a range of sand dunes, near the border with Algeria. It is accessible from Al Aweinat, about 80km (50 miles) away. Between Wadi Meggedet and Ghat, a particularly impressive and strange mountain of rock towers 1,281m (4,203ft) above the desert landscape. This is Kaf Ajnoun ('Mountain of Ghosts'), an evocative place associated with many Tuareg ghost stories (see pp16–17).

Al Aweinat (Serdeles)

Al Aweinat (Serdeles to the Tuareg) is the nearest town to the northern Jebel Acacus and most visitors to the Acacus pass through here on the way in or out. Al Aweinat is a small, sleepy town within a leafy oasis. There is nothing to do here, but there is a café and a camp if you are in need of a quick break or stopover. The only landmark building is a fort, a former castle during the early Arab period. It is now occupied by the Libyan police, so no visitors or photographs of the building are permitted.

Houn and Al Jufra

This area, approximately 350km (217 miles) northeast of Sebha, is too remote to attract many visitors. However, if you do happen to be driving all the way between the coast and the south, there are some interesting features to see in the Al Jufra region. It has a series of oasis towns – Sokha, Waddan and Houn – around which an abundance of dates and olives are cultivated. Houn is the site of an annual sweet-making festival (see p18). To the south, towards Sebha, the landscape shifts from sand dunes to dark rocks.

Southeast

This is the least visited part of the country and it is extremely remote. **Al Kufrah**, which has an airport, a post office, a hotel and a few eateries and shops, is the only town of any note. Parts of this area, such as the Tibesti region on the border with Chad, are closed to travellers for safety reasons (unexploded mines). However, there is some spectacular desert scenery in the southeast which can be visited. Most notable are the extinct volcano of Waw al-Namus and the Jebel al-Uweinat mountain range (see p121).

Drive: Desert experience

This route features the signature sights of southwest Libya, one of the most interesting regions in the country. Highlights along the route include traces of ancient civilisations in the form of rock art and the ancient capital of the Garamantian Empire. Another major highlight is the incredible and varied desert scenery, from the Ubari lakes to the rocky Acacus. You will need a guide to accompany you.

The distance covered varies considerably depending on the off-road route taken by the guide, but you will be travelling approximately 1,500km (930 miles). Allow a week in total, although adding a few extra days would make the trip more leisurely.

Start at Sebha. Follow the sealed road for about 150km (93 miles) southwest to Germa.

1 Germa

Stop off in Germa for a unique glimpse into the history of the region, which can be explored at the museum or at the archaeological site of Garama (*see p113*). The museum is located on the main road through town, near the petrol station. Garama (signed 'Old City') is about 1km (²/₃ mile) away from the main road, along a track opposite the petrol station.

Leave the main road and head into the desert to Wadi Methkandoush, about 150km (93 miles) from Germa.

2 Wadi Methkandoush

A tour of this dark stony valley is a good introduction to the region's prehistoric rock art. The landscape is not exactly picturesque, but it is the location of some of the oldest rock engravings in Libya.

Head south into the huge sand-sea of Idehan Murzuq and then curve round to the west to reach Wan Caza. Alternatively, if time is short, drive directly to Wan Caza.

3 Idehan Murzuq and Wan Caza

Wan Caza is much like a smaller version of Idehan Murzuq. Both have beautiful sand dunes and plenty of places to camp. After driving through flat and rocky types of desert scenery, the sand-sea makes a spectacular contrast. In addition to the beauty of the golden dunes, Wan Caza boasts panoramic Acacus views, giving you a glimpse of the next place on your tour.

The Jebel Acacus is to the west over the dunes of Wan Caza.

4 Jebel Acacus

Containing some of the world's best ancient cave art, the Jebel Acacus mountain range is evocative of a huge open-air sculpture park and gallery (*see p103*). This fantastic region merits two full days' exploration. Arriving from Wan Caza, you will be on the eastern edge of the Acacus, close to the main rock art area of Wadi Tashwinat. North of here is the scenic Awiss region.

Drive north through Awiss, rejoin the road at Al Aweinat (see p115) and go east back towards Germa. Shortly after passing through Germa, you will get to the village of Tekerkiba, which is the

gateway to the Ubari lakes. If need be, you can use toilets or showers or have a drink at one of three small camps in the village. Leave the road at Tekerkiba and head north into the dunes.

5 Ubari lakes

The Idehan Ubari, with its huge golden dunes and pretty oasis lakes, fringed by reeds, date palms and tamarisk trees, is another definitive highlight of the Libyan Sahara. The most scenic of the oases are Mavo, Gebraoun and Umm al-Maa (*see p110*).

Return south to rejoin the road at Tekerkiba and go east back to Sebha.

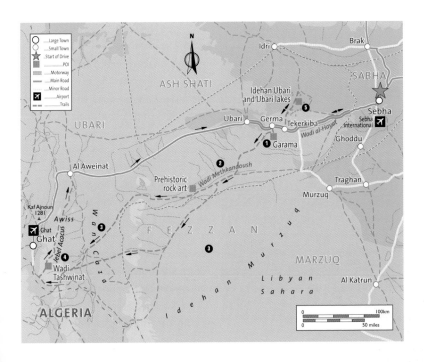

Desert ecosystem

The Sahara is a landscape of contradictions: fierce yet fragile, harsh and inhospitable yet uniquely beautiful and surprising. One of the most striking things about this most hostile of environments is how it can actually support life. Although Libya has a scarcity of wild mammals, a few species survive. Deep in the Libyan Sahara, gazelles, fennec foxes and waddan (a type of large deer similar to a mountain goat) roam the most remote areas, such as the far southeast and the far southwest. Species such as these have evolved to suit the desert's climate and are vital to its ecosystem. Sadly, several of the most iconic Saharan species, particularly gazelles, are critically endangered, and the region has already suffered the total loss of some species. In the last decade, Libya has joined 13 other North African states in agreeing to an action plan with the Convention on Migratory Species, aiming to restore habitats and reintroduce populations of Saharan antelopes. Whether this will be successful in reversing the decline remains to be seen.

Smaller creatures such as lizards, rodents, snakes, beetles and scorpions are more common. The snakes that are present are the Saharan sand snake, the striped sand snake and the horned viper. Travellers are unlikely to come across any of them, particularly as they rarely emerge in the winter months. A few migratory birds, frequent visitors to northern Libya, stray down to the south. The black and white moula moula bird is a more consistent desert resident. It is described by the Tuareg as a messenger bird, associated with delivering happiness.

The main domestic animals are camels and goats, which are able to

A snake trail in the sand

Goats are not put off by the thorny acacia tree

eat the thorny leaves of the acacia tree. In addition to the acacia, which can survive in the driest areas, little clumps of grass provide surprising bursts of fresh green in the midst of all the sand. There is a more interesting selection of plants in and around oases. Date palms are the most widespread and iconic of the oasis trees, while tall reeds typically line the shores of the lakes. Other vegetation includes fig and oleander trees.

The desert can be very windy, blowing loose grains of sand up into the air, but the dunes of the sand-seas are effectively unwavering. A natural wonder, these mountainous dunes have been forming since the dawn of the Sahara as a desert. The shape of their ridges reveals the prevailing direction of the wind. Rain does occasionally fall in the desert and when it does, it can feel like an almost magical experience. Even relatively short bursts of rain can significantly cool the sand and transform its appearance. The usual soft yellow of the dunes gives way to darker, layered tones that evoke melting butter, with marble-like swirling patterns. Desert plants seem to be sheltering under the surface, waiting for an opportunity to grow, and after the rain the sand in some areas becomes suddenly carpeted in green grasses and bushes. Unlikely as it seems, some of the most barren areas, such as Wadi Methkandoush, are vulnerable to the odd flash-flood.

Getting away from it all

While nowhere in Libya really ever feels overcrowded, the Sahara is the ideal place to get away from civilisation altogether. Travel just a short distance from the nearest town and it immediately seems like the middle of nowhere. Some of the most beautiful places are also the most remote. Vast swathes of sand cocoon you in an environment that is serenely quiet and still. For those sticking to the coastal regions, there are ways to relax and experience different aspects of the country between visits to the great sites.

In the desert

Any trip into the desert is a chance to get away from it all. The suggestions below represent just some of the many ways to relax or leave the world behind in the Libyan Sahara.

See the sights from a 'ship of the desert'

Camel tours

Travelling by camel-back instead of by 4WD is a fantastic way to slow down your pace and forego the modern world. Naturally, you will not be able to see as much of the desert as you would in a 4WD, but you will get to experience the area you do see in more depth and in an age-old way. Camels also have better green credentials than cars! Although most desert trips are by car, it should be possible to design an itinerary where most or some of the travel is by camel. One company offering this as an option is Arkno Tours (*see p130*), who can arrange a camel safari in the amazing Jebel Acacus region. For those not wanting to spend days on camel-back, short camel rides may be available in some places, such as Ghadames. Talk to your tour company about possibilities.

Desert swimming

Arguably the best spot for a desert swim is Umm al-Maa, the prettiest of the

Reeds and date palms surrounding Umm al-Maa lake

Ubari lakes. It is impossible to swim properly in oasis lakes, as the high salt content of the water renders it much like a flotation pool. The feeling of bobbing around on the surface in the midst of palm trees and sand dunes is certainly special. Of course, at the end of this relaxing experience you will be covered in salt, so before taking the plunge, make sure you think about when you will next be able to have a shower.

Idehan Murzuq

The dunes of Murzuq sand-sea are similar to those of the better-known Ubari sand-sea, but on an even grander scale. Murzuq is less visited than the Ubari lakes area, so it offers a truly remote sand dune experience (*see p112*). This is less a sand-sea than a sand mountain range, with peaks and valleys. Surveying it all from one of the

peaks, you can feel like there is nothing in the world except shimmering sand and nobody on the planet except the members of your group.

The remote southeast: Waw al-Namus and Jebel al-Uweinat

The appeals of this part of the Sahara for some travellers are the dramatic scenery and the opportunity to visit somewhere that is well and truly removed from the beaten track. Few visitors venture out to this region, where there are just a few remote towns in a vast expanse of desert. The southeast's two biggest attractions are Waw al-Namus and Jebel al-Uweinat.

The extinct volcano of **Waw al-Namus** is one of the most astonishing landscapes in Libya. The sand around the crater is black, speckled in places with green crystallised grains of lava.

Gorgeous blue seas near Apollonia

Even more extraordinary are the three oasis lakes in the area, with their jewel-coloured blue, green and red waters. Factor in the palm trees that border the lakes and it adds up to a striking colour palette. Unsurprisingly, there is no accommodation anywhere near Waw al-Namus, so camping is the only option. Avoid sleeping too near the crater or lakes as this is mosquito territory. Waw al-Namus is 300km (186 miles) away from civilisation (in the form of the nearest small towns), so it makes for quite an epic journey by 4WD to reach it.

Even deeper into Libya's southeastern corner is the rocky **Jebel al-Uweinat** mountain range, which straddles Libya's borders with Egypt and Sudan (although neither border is open here). This is the region's answer to the Jebel Acacus in the southwest, but much less visited. There is a wealth of ancient art sites concealed among the incredible rock formations, with representations of human and animal figures. This area is also quite rich in desert wildlife.

The remote southwest:
Wadi Meggedet

A little-visited part of the remote southwest, this area is still home to desert animals like the gazelle, fennec fox and waddan. It also has an otherworldly landscape, with incredible rock formations rising out of the sand at all angles (*see p115*).

At the beach

Despite Libya's long Mediterranean coastline, it is far from a beach holiday destination. This means that, with the exception of Fridays when Libyan families tend to visit the seaside, there are miles of uncrowded beaches. To avoid feeling uncomfortable in this conservative culture, women should either cover up as much as possible or choose a secluded spot where there is no-one else around. Many of the coastal sites have decent beaches either on site or nearby. Particularly scenic seaside areas include the stretch of coastline to the west of Sabratha, and the northern tip of Cyrenaica.

Farwa Island

Tiny Farwa Island is just a few kilometres from the mainland and can be reached by ferry from Bu Kammash, a small town near the border with Tunisia. The island is covered in palm trees, broken only by the occasional village or sand dune. On the north side there is a pristine beach.

Ras al-Hammamah

The route from Al Bayda (*see p83*) down to the coast at Ras al-Hammamah is a scenic drive of about 23km (14 miles). As you descend the winding road to the seafront, a row of sandy coves appears, the white sand and blue sea contrasting brilliantly with the green hills. There is a tourist village at Ras al-Hammamah, which is popular with local families but can also be used by travellers.

West of Sabratha

The far northwest coast of Libya, between Sabratha and the Tunisian border, is characterised by lovely white-sand beaches. Few itineraries feature this area as there are no sites of real significance, but it does have great potential for relaxing on a quiet beach. It is also possible to detour to one of the beaches within the same day as a visit to Sabratha.

Ras al-Hammamah's rocky shoreline

In the mountains
Jebel al-Akhdar region

There is a possibility that, after some time in Libya, sand is the one thing you will really want to get away from. Another possibility is that after exploring the cities and sites, you might want to spend some time in the countryside. The Jebel al-Akhdar region, in Cyrenaica, is the only significant forested area in the country and it has some stunning scenery.

Positioned as it is between a glorious bay and the lush hills of the mountains, **Ras al-Hillal** (*see p82*) would be a serious contender for the title of most scenically located village in Libya. Nature really takes centre stage here, with a stunning display of colours. Red and purple wild flowers tumble over the rocks by the azure sea. Inland, the landscape remains striking, with a vividly contrasting palette of red earth and trees such as myrtle and juniper.

Wadi al-Kuf ('Valley of Caves') is an especially picturesque part of Cyrenaica. The main valley is crossed by tributaries and framed by wooded cliffs. The slopes are indented with numerous caves. There are panoramic, if slightly dizzying, views from a bridge which takes the main road across one of the side valleys. You can access the main valley by a smaller winding road that loops down and back up to the main road. Wadi al-Kuf has a dramatic history, as one of the key places where local resistance fighters battled the Italian army in 1927.

Ras al-Hillal

Jebel Nafusa region

The main reason to visit the Jebel Nafusa is to see the old Berber architecture. However, this mountainous region also boasts some amazing landscapes. Near the town of Jadu, there are a number of natural springs. One of these is **Ain az-Zarqa**, about 5km (3 miles) southwest of Jadu. It is like a little oasis, a palm-lined pool bordered by cliffs. There is a picnic spot near the top of the cliffs, from where a road leads down to the pool. This is quite a long walk, but you can also look down on the oasis from above, taking special care near the edge.

In the city

Tripoli and Benghazi both have attractive green spaces in the centre of town. On hot days, city-dwellers lounge in the shade of the trees, contributing to the laidback atmosphere. One good way to take a break from touring is to spend a bit of time without your guide, just meandering around Tripoli. The harbour, the medina and Algeria Square are all good spots to sit back and watch the world go by. Alternatively, check out one of the hammams in the medina. For a minimal charge you can get a massage, steam bath or body scrub. Typical opening hours are between 8am and 3pm and there are different days for men and women (*see pp163–4*).

Al-Saraya Restaurant/Café in Tripoli

When to go

Libya is a northern hemisphere country and experiences seasons across broadly the same months of the year as in Europe and North America, although less distinctively. In summer it gets very hot across the country, and in the desert, temperatures really soar. For this reason, the peak tourist season in Libya runs during the cooler months, from October to early May.

Coastal trips

The climate of Libya's coastal regions is essentially Mediterranean. Summers are hot and balmy and winters are cooler but rarely cold, apart from in the mountains. Tripolitania tends to be warmer than Cyrenaica, where there is more of a breeze. Average coastal summer temperatures tend to peak around 30°C (86°F). Winter temperatures are usually in the 15–20°C (59–68°F) range. It can be rainy in the winter months, but rarely in the summer. The Jebel al-Akhdar region sees the most rain, and very occasionally some snow even falls. Spring and autumn have the most pleasant weather, although in Tripolitania there is a risk of sporadic spring sandstorms. A dusty, oppressive wind known as *ghibli* can blow in from the Sahara, bringing desert heat with it. It is possible to visit the coastal areas at any time of year, although summer is definitely the low season.

Desert trips

The best times of year to visit the Libyan Sahara are autumn (October and November) or spring (March, April and early May). At these times it is usually warm but not sweltering. Excursions into the desert should definitely be avoided in the summer, when temperatures around 40°C (104°F) are typical and even 50°C (122°F) is not uncommon. Trips in winter (December through February) are fine, but while daytime temperatures should feel comfortable, it gets very cold at night, often dipping below freezing.

Islamic and national holidays

Libya has a number of national holidays in addition to the holidays of the Islamic calendar. The national holidays happen at the same time each year (*see p153*). Religious holidays are set according to the lunar calendar and hence vary from year to year (*see p33*). Travellers should be particularly aware of the holy month of Ramadan (*see below*) and the Day of Mourning on 26 October. The latter, a day of remembrance for Libyans who died during the Italian occupation, is marked with a temporary isolation from the outside world. International phone lines are cut off and borders and airports are closed for the day. On other national holidays many businesses will be closed.

Travelling during Ramadan

The holy month of Ramadan, when Muslims observe a complete fast during daylight hours, can be a tricky time to travel in Libya. Restaurants in popular areas often open exclusively for tourists, and Libyans will not be offended by non-Muslims eating, but extra forward-planning around when and where to eat is advisable. Itineraries may also be slightly affected as opening hours during Ramadan may be different from normal. Your tour

company should be able to give specific advice. Ramadan falls during the months of August and September in 2009 and 2010 (*see p33*).

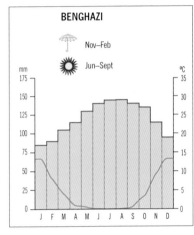

BENGHAZI
Nov–Feb
Jun–Sept

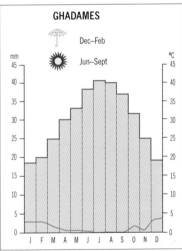

GHADAMES
Dec–Feb
Jun–Sept

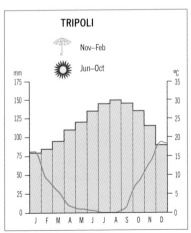

TRIPOLI
Nov–Feb
Jun–Oct

WEATHER CONVERSION CHART

25.4mm = 1 inch

°F = 1.8 × °C + 32

Getting around

Orientation is difficult for non-Arabic speakers because most signs are only in Arabic, but the practicalities of getting around are almost always taken care of by tour companies. Travellers typically travel by cars, tour buses and domestic flights, rarely using public transport. Desert passes from the Libyan authorities are required for all excursions into the Sahara. Your tour operator should arrange this.

Getting around the cities

Libya's city centres are small and manageable to walk around. Aside from crossing roads, the main challenge is finding places when you cannot read the street signs. Landmarks will help. Private taxis (marked black and white) are widely available. Ask your guide or hotel to write down where you want to go so that you can show the driver.

Driving

The best news about driving in Libya is that petrol is extremely cheap. Sealed roads are generally fine, but there are hazards, including everything from drivers doing U-turns on dual carriageways to camels and sand straying onto the road. Off-road desert driving requires a 4WD. The speed limit varies according to the type of road: 50km/h (31mph) in towns; 70km/h (43mph) on small rural roads; 85km/h (53mph) on main routes outside towns; and 100km/h (62mph) on highways. Libyan drivers pay little attention to speed limits. Drive on the right side of the road.

If you bring your own car or rent a car, a representative of the tour company that arranged your visit will have to travel with you, which is useful for navigation. You will also need an array of documentation if bringing your own vehicle. Contact an automobile association in your home country to ask about a vehicle passport and international driving permit. When you arrive in Libya you will have to temporarily join the Automobile and Touring Club of Libya and buy local number plates, although you can return these for a partial refund. Few tourists rent cars as tour companies arrange cars with drivers, but there are branches of **Europcar** (*www.europcar-libya.com*) in the **Corinthia Bab Africa Hotel** (*Tel: (021) 335 1990*) and at the **International Airport** (*Tel: (022) 634 950*).

There are police and military road checkpoints throughout Libya,

A jeep convoy in the desert at Acacus

which may check passports or tour itineraries.

Automobile and Touring Club of Libya, Sharia Sayedy, Tripoli.

Tel: (021) 360 5986. Fax: (021) 360 5866.

Public transport

The public transport options within towns are mini-buses and shared taxis. Both are painted white and yellow. There are no bus stations or timetables, but town centres have car park areas where the buses and taxis wait for passengers. Unless already full, they will also stop on the street if signalled. An-Nakhl as-Seria and Al-Itihad al-Afriqi operate inter-city bus services, with main depots in Tripoli and Benghazi. Comfort is variable, but fares are reasonable.

Domestic flights

Libya has two domestic airlines: Al-Buraq Air and Libyan Arab Airlines. The main routes are between Tripoli, Benghazi and Sebha. There are less frequent flights to and from small airports at Lebreq (Al Bayda) and Al Kufrah. The remote towns of Tobruk, Ghadames, Ghat and Houn also have airports, but flight routes are frequently closed. Tour guides are usually charged with check-in, but you need to identify your luggage on the runway and ensure it gets put on the plane.

Border crossings

The only borders open to travellers are those with Egypt and Tunisia near the coast. Both are straightforward to get to and cross. Your Libyan tour company will typically arrange for you to be picked up and/or dropped off at the border. There are also long-distance buses between Benghazi, Alexandria and Cairo and between Tripoli and Tunis.

TOUR OPERATORS

In addition to tour companies within Libya, a number of European companies offer tours in conjunction with Libyan partners. There are far fewer North American or Australian companies featuring tours to Libya, so travellers from these countries may choose to book with UK-based companies. In Libya itself, there are many excellent and knowledgeable tour guides. A few individual guides who specialise in tours of particular sites are recommended in the destination guide chapters in this book. Tour companies should be able to contact them or other specialists for you.

In Libya
Arkno Tours
Extensive choice of group and tailor-made tours throughout the country. The UK office is a great source of information.
38 Sharia Abd al-Rahman al-Kawakabi, Garden City, Tripoli.
Tel: (+218 21) 444 4044.
Email: info@arkno.com. www.arkno.com
1–3 Love Lane, Woolwich, London SE18 6QT. Tel: (+44 2088) 556 373.
Email: info@arknouk.com
Magic Libya Incoming & Tours
Specialists in desert tours.
Libya Head Office, Tripoli.
Tel: (+218 21) 340 8355/732/731.
Fax: (+218 21) 340 8355.

Rugged jeeps can ferry you around in relative comfort

Email: info@magic-dmc.com.
www.magiclibya.biz

In the UK

When dialling from within the UK, drop
the +44 and add a 0 before the area code.

Andante Travels

Archaeological tours led by specialist
lecturers.

Tel: (+44 1722) 713 800.
www.andantetravels.co.uk

Arab Tours

Tours and flights.

60 Marylebone Lane, London W1U 2NZ.
Tel: (+44 2079) 353 273.
Fax: (+44 2074) 864 237.
Email: arabtours@btconnect.com.
www.arabtours.co.uk

Audley Travel

Specialists in tailor-made tours plus
occasional group tours.

Tel: (+44 1993) 838 400.
www.audleytravel.com

Captain's Choice

Luxury cruises plus charter flights.

Tel: (+44 845) 603 5764.
www.captainschoice.co.uk

The Classic Traveller

Tripoli city-break specialists.

Tel: (+44 800) 988 5822.
www.theclassictraveller.co.uk

Holt's Battlefield Tours

Specialists in battlefield tours.

Tel: (+44 845) 375 0430. www.holts.co.uk

National Geographic Journeys

Lecturer-led tours of the Roman and
Greek sites and the desert.

Tel: (+44 800) 988 5175.
www.ngjourneys.co.uk

Oasis Overland

Specialists in overland adventure travel.

Tel: (+44 1963) 363 400.
www.oasisoverland.co.uk

Pettitts

Specialists in tailor-made travel.

Tel: (+44 1892) 515 966.
www.pettitts.co.uk

Silk Road and Beyond

Specialists in tailor-made holidays.

Tel: (+44 2073) 713 131.
www.silkroadandbeyond.co.uk

Silk Steps

Specialists in tailor-made tours.

Tel: (+44 1278) 722 460.
www.silksteps.co.uk

Special Tours

Specialists in art and cultural tours.

Tel: (+44 2077) 302 297.
www.specialtours.co.uk

Titan HiTours

Group tours of the Roman and Greek
cities.

Tel: (+44 800) 988 5805.
www.titanhitours.co.uk

Western Desert Battlefield Tours

Specialists in battlefield tours.

Tel: (+44 1283) 526 588.
www.western-desert.de

In the USA and Canada

Eldertreks

Specialists in tours for the over-50s.

Tel: (+1 416) 588 5000/800 741 7956.
www.eldertreks.com

Odysseys Unlimited

Tours for small groups.

Tel: (+1 617) 454 9100/1 888 370 6765.
www.odysseys-unlimited.com

Hotels and accommodation

Libya's hospitality industry is developing fast and there is now a good choice of hotels in the north of the country. Hotels can be divided into two main categories: newer privately run establishments and older government-owned stalwarts. The private hotels, most of which fit in the mid-range price bracket, tend to be the best choice for value and quality. In the south, outside of Sebha, camping is the main form of accommodation and a fantastic way to experience the Sahara.

Desert camping

For a really memorable experience, camping in the desert is hard to beat. It is also essentially the only form of accommodation available in the Libyan Sahara. However, you will still have a degree of choice over how to camp. You can choose a permanent or seasonal camp, or you can plan an itinerary with your tour company and sleep out in the open desert wherever you find a good spot.

Sleeping out in the open under the desert stars is certainly recommended from an adventurous point of view. It is also surprisingly easy to organise, as the tour company should bring along all the tents, sleeping bags and other necessary equipment. They will also take care of food, usually by including a well-stocked kitchen car and a cook in the expedition party. An added piece of good news for open desert campers is that mosquitoes are rarely encountered away from the oases. If your desert trip is in the winter months, make sure you are prepared for cold overnight temperatures.

Permanent camps can be found in the oasis towns of Al Aweinat (Serdeles), Germa, Ghat, Sebha, Tekerkiba and Ubari. They have simple huts to sleep in, shared bathrooms

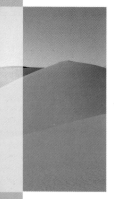

A suite at the Zumit Hotel in Tripoli, with a view over the Arch of Marcus Aurelius

Magic Lodge camp at Ubari lakes

with showers, and eating areas. The main problem with this option is that mosquitoes swarm around the oases at night. Even if you are not staying in one, the camps can be good places to take a shower or rest in the shade at lunchtime.

The final option is semi-permanent camps, which are set up for the length of the season by individual tour companies. For travellers who want the experience of desert camping, but with increased comfort, these are the perfect solution. They offer relative luxury by desert standards. Expect tents on raised platforms, complete with beds and little bathrooms. Communal tents are also set up for socialising and eating. All in all, the seasonal camps are attractive and more comfortable than the permanent camps.

Whatever type of camping trip you choose, make sure you are sensitive to the fragility of the desert environment. Keep showers as short as possible and do not leave any rubbish behind. If there are no litter bins, take rubbish with you, although tissue paper can be buried if need be.

Hotels

As a rule, the mid-range private hotels in Libya are comfortable, agreeable and welcoming places to stay, offering great value for money. They are still relative newcomers to the country's accommodation scene and have provided a welcome alternative to the government-owned hotels that used to dominate the sector. There are still government hotels operating, but the private hotels are essentially a much better option all round. Most are similar to each other in terms of design and facilities. It is standard for private bathrooms, air conditioning and breakfast to be included in the room rate.

Hotels that offer really unique character are not numerous, but there are a few notable examples in the top-end category. The Corinthia Bab Africa (*see p161*), Libya's only five-star hotel at the time of writing, provides a standout level of luxury with uniquely designed details throughout. The Dar Ghadames (*see p170*) and Zumit (*see pp161–2*) hotels have both been creatively furnished in the traditional style of their local areas

The stylish Corinthia Hotel, Tripoli

(Ghadames and Tripoli's medina respectively).

Libya has very few hotels in the budget category, so there is a gap between the mid-range options and the hostels (*see below*). However, the reasonable pricing of the mid-range hotels goes some way towards making up for this shortfall. Hotel bookings are generally made through the tour company. However, it may be possible for your tour company to accommodate any specific requests. This will depend on the individual company and on the size of group you are travelling with. Very few hotels outside the top-end bracket have websites. Another point to note is that hotels will generally hold on to your passport for the duration of your stay.

Hostels

For cheap accommodation within some of the towns and cities, Libya has a network of youth hostels. The central contact for these is the Libyan Youth Hostel Association. Accommodation is usually in dormitory rooms with shared bathrooms. Separate rooms for women are common. Single female travellers may feel more comfortable travelling as part of a group because, away from the hotels routinely used by tour groups, there is more of a tendency for local men to stare at women. Another budget option is to camp in the grounds of a hotel or hostel that welcomes campers, as some do. There is usually a small charge for the space and use of facilities.

WHAT CLOTHES TO BRING

Although Libya is a conservative society, travellers are not expected to abide by the same sets of social rules as the locals. However, women should generally aim to cover their legs and shoulders. Swimming costumes should ideally be covered up as much as possible on the beach, to avoid offending sensibilities or attracting unwanted stares. Headscarves are unnecessary, except as a mark of respect when visiting mosques. A light scarf can come in handy for everything from mosque visits to sun protection. Everyone must remove shoes before entering mosques. Desert trip essentials include cool loose-fitting clothing (shorts are OK in remote areas), covered shoes, a hat and warm clothes for winter nights.

Libyan Youth Hostel Association. Based in Tripoli's central Buyut ash-Shabaab hostel, 69 Sharia Amr ibn al-Ass, Tripoli. Tel/fax: (021) 333 0118.

Tourist villages

Libya has a number of coastal tourist villages (*qaryat as-siyahe*), which are usually located right on the shore. The name is a little misleading as these are marketed at Libyans, but foreign travellers can make bookings through their tour operators. They are very popular with Libyan families in the summer months, but at other times of the year, rooms tend to be more readily available. Tourist villages vary in quality, but some are excellent. They usually have self-catering villas and a range of amenities on site, including restaurants, shops, play areas and leisure facilities.

Food and drink

The ceremony of eating is an important part of the Libyan culture. Drinking is much less so, although the traditional tea houses are an exception to this rule. Libya has lots of fantastic restaurants, but the culinary industry often does not do justice to the tradition of adventurous and varied home-cooking. You may end up eating the same dishes repeatedly, although as these are generally tasty and filling, on a short visit this is unlikely to be cause for complaint.

Specialities

Libyan cuisine varies between regions, but the basic staples of the main course are couscous, rice and sometimes macaroni or other types of pasta. Meat (generally lamb, mutton or chicken) is the centrepiece of the meal. Fish and seafood dishes are available in many coastal restaurants, while camel is a logical choice for desert meals. Libyan food tends to be delicately spiced rather than overtly spicy, and many sauces are tomato-based. A classic starter that features in many restaurants is *sharba Libya* (Libyan soup). This hearty broth is traditionally made with lamb, orzo pasta (although couscous can be substituted), spices, herbs and lemon in a rich tomato sauce. Other savoury highlights include *algarra* (seafood or lamb, tomato, peppers and herbs slow-cooked in an amphora), *fitaat* (wheat pancakes filled with lentils and mutton and covered in sauce) and *taajeelah* (traditional Tuareg flatbread). *Algarra* is served in some restaurants, including Al Athar in Tripoli (*see pp162–3*). *Fitaat* features on the traditional menu at some of the houses in Ghadames (*see pp86–7*). And Tuareg bread is prepared and baked in the open kitchen of the desert, using sand heated by a fire as an outdoor oven.

Sweet treats

Libya has plenty of edible delights of a sweeter nature, from the ubiquitous dates to a range of desserts, which are similar to those found in other countries of the Middle East and North Africa. Typically, they are a cross between sweets, pastries and cakes, featuring nuts and honey. One speciality is *shamiya*, a crumbly sesame-flavoured sweet, sometimes topped with pistachios. There are many patisseries in Libya, but Tripoli's Alharate and the Oriental Corner (*p162*) are worth mentioning.

Restaurants

Some restaurants have quite long menus, while others basically have

Dates are part of a traditional dessert

specials of the day. Choice tends to be limited in smaller restaurants, but staff will do their best to accommodate dietary requirements (*see* '*Vegetarians*', *p138*). A typical Libyan restaurant meal consists of a feast of courses, usually bread and dips to start, followed by soup, salad (which may be one salad or a selection from a buffet), a main course, dessert and coffee or tea. You will certainly not leave hungry!

Libyan cuisine has absorbed various international influences, from Arab countries, Turkey and the Mediterranean, and many chefs are originally from other countries. Dedicated international restaurants specialising in particular cuisines are hard to find, however. Some exceptions include the restaurants at the Corinthia Hotel (*see p163*) and the Turkish restaurants of Benghazi (*see p168*).

Shopping and markets

The supermarkets in Tripoli have by far the best range of groceries. Options are more limited in smaller towns, but there is generally at least one store selling a range of dried and canned foods and some bread, cheeses and fruit. If you are self-catering or packing for a picnic, it is worth thinking ahead and stocking up in Tripoli or asking for local advice about what will be available at your destination. For example, bread can sometimes be hard to come by in Ghadames, but the small town of Bughilan, near Gharyan, has a roadside bakery. Fresh produce, such as honey, seasonal fruit and olive oil, can often be bought from stalls along the main routes through the country.

Just south of Tripoli's medina, on Sharia ar-Rashid, is a collection of enticing food markets selling produce from fish and meat to fruit, olives and spices. Head to the fruit or deli-style stalls for a quick snack, or linger in the spice market, where big open sacks of ground and whole spices, dried pulses and lentils make for a vivid display. Meanwhile, the large fish market just east of Tripoli has a wide choice of the rich pickings to be had from the Mediterranean. You can buy a fish there and have it cooked at a nearby restaurant (*see, for example, Barakoda Restaurant listing, p165*).

Vegetarians

Visiting vegetarians need to be prepared to be looked on as an oddity. However, Libyans are starting to encounter vegetarianism more often as tourism increases. Restaurants will do their best to prepare you something, although the level of imagination employed may vary. Some restaurants even have meat-free options on their menus, often pasta dishes. It is important to inform your tour company in advance of exactly what you do not eat (be specific), especially for desert trips, when food is carried in specially. When visiting restaurants, always explain as soon as you arrive. Some non-meat highlights include lentil soup, often served as an alternative to Libyan soup, and spiced couscous or pasta dishes with chickpeas or vegetables. Appetisers are usually vegetarian-friendly because of the popularity of salads and the interesting breads. The cheese bread at Matam Turki in Benghazi (*see p167*) is worth a special mention.

Drinks

Alcohol is illegal in Libya and this prohibition is taken very seriously, to the point where bars on planes and ships must be sealed as they approach the country. Do not attempt to bring any alcoholic drinks into Libya. Although the tap water is technically potable, it should be avoided to safeguard against potential stomach upsets. Bottled water is widely available, along with canned soft drinks. There is not much choice of more interesting drinks, although some restaurants offer non-alcoholic beers and a bright red fizzy concoction called *masabiyah Jamaica*, which is a mixture of 7-Up, Coke and Mirinda. Fresh smoothies and milkshakes are found in a few places, among them Benghazi's lively Souq al-Jreed and the lobby café at the sophisticated Corinthia Hotel in Tripoli. Tea and coffee are popular beverages and mint tea is a particular highlight, served from Tripoli's tea houses to Tuareg tents in the Sahara (*see p140*).

Restaurant Athar near the Arch of Marcus Aurelius in Tripoli

Entertainment

Entertainment options in Libya are extremely limited and you should be prepared to slow down in the evenings. Home entertainments like satellite TV, CDs, DVDs and computer games are popular with Libyans, as are home-based family gatherings. In the desert, you have to make your own entertainment, but chatting around a fire, reading a book or possibly enjoying music and songs with the Tuareg are not bad ways to pass an evening.

In the cities, aside from lingering over a long meal, there is little to do except drink tea and soak up the evening atmosphere. After the languorous heat of the day (particularly in the summer months), outdoor spaces such as parks and tea gardens do come alive at night and are great places to relax and people-watch.

Tea houses and gardens

Libyan men tend to socialise in tea houses, while Libyan women are typically more likely to stay indoors or visit each other at home, unless they are out with their families. Men often linger for hours over their tea or coffee, playing games like chess or cards and sometimes smoking water pipes (called *sheesha* or *nargila*). Although the atmosphere in many tea houses is very male-dominated, there are some where women can feel welcome. This is most likely in cosmopolitan Tripoli. Tea houses stay open late and are popular throughout the afternoon and evening. In Tripoli, the most atmospheric areas are around Green Square and Algeria Square (*for detailed listings of specific tea houses, see pp162 & 164–5*).

Tea drinking is an integral part of the Libyan culture of hospitality. Visitors are likely to be offered tea throughout the country, whether in a tent in the desert, in a traditional house in Ghadames or Gharyan, or in a Tripolitanian hotel. Sociable tea drinking can involve a fascinating sense of ceremony. Traditionally, everyone sits on cushions around a low table, where the host prepares and pours several rounds of tea for the guests. The first round is strong, sweet and frothy, the second is flavoured with fresh mint, and the third is poured over peanuts and almonds. In tea houses there is often a choice of these to order. Tea is generally brewed in an elaborate teapot and served in little glasses.

Live music and dance

Traditional Libyan music and dance performances are often of Berber or

Tuareg origin. Performances can be enjoyed at local festivals, notably those at Ghadames, Ghat, Kabaw and Zuara (*see pp18–19*). Typically, festivals and weddings are the only times ritualistic dances are performed, but there are local dance troupes in Ghadames who re-enact celebratory dances during the high season (October to April). You can ask in town for details of where performances are taking place. Traditional dances vary from region to region, but are often danced in circles with rhythmical clapping or chanting. Instrumental accompaniment is usually simple, with wind instruments and drums being popular. Some restaurants and hotels, particularly in Tripoli, feature atmospheric live music in the evenings. Athar Restaurant, Essaa Restaurant and the Corinthia Bab Africa Hotel are among those that stand out (*see pp161–3*).

Café in the Zumit Hotel courtyard

Shopping

Shopping in Libya is a really enjoyable pastime. The atmosphere at most shopping areas is unhurried and friendly, and there is an assortment of unusual crafts to choose from. Tripoli's souks undoubtedly offer the best variety, and wandering around the medina picking out souvenirs can be a great way to end a holiday. Shopping highlights elsewhere in the country include buying crafts from the Tuareg in the Sahara and finding items that are specialities of particular places.

Prices, etiquette and practicalities

Bargaining, or haggling, is generally not done in Libya, especially in shops, where things almost always have a fixed (and reasonable) price. There is sometimes more scope for negotiation at stalls, most notably with the Tuareg craftsmen in the desert. Prices are likely to seem rather low to travellers, although many of the jewellery shops in Tripoli cater quite specifically to the local wedding gift market, rather than to the casual souvenir buyer. Typical shopping hours are 10am–2pm & 5–8pm, Saturdays to Thursdays. A few shops also open on Friday evenings.

Tripoli's souks

The best places to shop for distinctive souvenirs and gifts are the souks of Tripoli's medina. Although there are shops scattered throughout the medina, most of the interesting ones are concentrated in the southeastern quarter, near the Green Square entrance. The atmospheric Copper Souk (Souq al-Ghizdir) is a definite highlight. This narrow alley to the side of the Ottoman clock tower is crammed with metalworks, from lanterns to tea sets to crescents destined for the tops of minarets. The shops are open-fronted and double as forges, so you can see the craftsmen at work. They will sometimes take commissions, which you can pick up a few days later. Elsewhere in the medina, jewellery, rugs, cushions and clothing are among the traditionally made items. There are several very interesting shops along Souq al-Attara and Souq al-Turk.

Shopping in the Sahara

Tuareg craftsmen can generally be found at all the major desert sites in the tourist season (usually October to mid-May). In some places, such as the Ubari lakes, they set up semi-permanent markets, and you are also likely to encounter individual traders along roadsides or at desert camps. The range of items for sale tends to be much the same from place to place and typically includes an eye-catching array of jewellery and ornaments. Silver is the most commonly used material, but there are also items made of bronze, leather and sandstone. The jewellery pieces are ornately decorated and often marked with symbols, such as the Tuareg cross (*see p17*) or Tuareg Tifinagh alphabet, making them unique Saharan souvenirs. Some of the artisans also make delicate miniature silver or bronze statues of desert animals. Other items you may see include camel-skin bowls, sandstone figures, leather pouches and silver daggers with decorative leather hilts. For those not going deep into the desert, Tuareg crafts are also sold in some of the shops in Tripoli and in Ghadames.

Unique souvenirs

Certain regional crafts deserve a particular mention for their unique character. Ghadames is known for its embroidered slippers and boots, which are characterised by their vivid colours and intricate patterns. There are a few residents still making these in the

A Tuareg jewellery stall at the Magic Lodge in Acacus

traditional way, including the Bin
Yeddar family. Their workshop is
located in the small parade of shops
near the museum. Ghadames is also a
good place to pick up palm-woven
crafts. There is a long tradition in the
town of putting palm trees to creative
and functional use (*see p89*). Ghat
offers a different sort of shopping
experience at a weekly open-air market
on Tuesdays. Clothes are the main
focus, with Tuareg turbans and baggy
trousers among the garments on sale.
For pottery, Gharyan (*see pp98–9*) is
undoubtedly the place to go. At the
main roadside market on the outskirts
of the town there is an extensive choice
of decorative bowls, vases and other
items. Rug-weaving is another very
traditional craft, especially among the
Berbers. Although the number of
weavers working in the traditional way
has reportedly fallen in recent years,
there is still a good selection of rugs on
display in Tripoli and other towns in
Tripolitania. In Benghazi, the Acacus
House (*see p64*) is worth a visit for
anyone interested in picking up an
original work by a Libyan sculptor.
The gallery/gift shop space (which
doubles as the artist's home) is
crammed with wooden carvings
in various sizes.

Books and information
The best shops for books in English are
Tripoli's **Fergiani's Bookshop** (on
Sharia 1 September) and **Fergiani 2
Bookshop** (on Sharia Mirza). Both are

THE GREEN BOOK

The Green Book is an aptly named volume (the cover is dark green) containing Colonel Qaddafi's views and visions on subjects as diverse as economics and gender differences. He wrote it in the 1970s during a retreat in the desert, to outline his 'Third Universal Theory' and ultimately offer 'a solution to the problem of democracy'. For the benefit of those curious to read Qaddafi's philosophies on life, politics and everything, *The Green Book* has been translated into 84 languages and can be found in Fergiani's Bookshop (*see below*) and at some tourist sites. Catchy extracts, such as 'partners not wage workers', also appear on posters and banners all over Libya.

open 10am–2pm & 5–9pm on
Saturdays to Thursdays, and 5–9pm on
Fridays. They have a great range,
whether you are after glossy coffee-
table books with beautiful photographs
of the Sahara, novels or language
books. Fergiani's is generally a good
source of information and souvenirs.
They also sell postcards and copies of
The Green Book (*see box*) in several
languages. The Jamahiriya Museum gift
shop has a selection of maps, postcards
and guidebooks to Libya's major
attractions. Books about some of the
ancient sites, such as Leptis Magna and
Cyrene, can also be found at the sites
themselves and are generally available
in several European languages,
including English. At Leptis Magna,
there are a few souvenir shops located
around the main site car park. Cyrene
has a similar cluster of stalls just
outside the exit from the site (the
northern gate).

Souvenirs for sale at a souk in Tripoli

Sport and leisure

'Potential' is a word likely to spring to many visitors' minds when thinking about sport and leisure activities in Libya. With such a long Mediterranean coastline, rugged hills and vast expanses of sand dunes, there is much potential for enjoying the great outdoors. However, activity breaks are uncommon in the still-nascent tourism industry. It may be worth consulting your tour company as activities that are not routinely offered can sometimes be arranged.

Dune skiing

Dune skiing has not exactly taken off as a common pastime in the Libyan Sahara, but the enterprising owners of the camp at Gebraoun, one of the Ubari lakes, have spotted an opportunity. You can rent skis or a snowboard there at a small charge. The dunes around the lake vary in size, so you can tailor the activity to suit your level. Remember to take care as the infrastructure and support of ski stations does not exist in the deepest Sahara!

Swimming

Although swimming is unlikely to be top of your agenda when you visit the Libyan coastline (given all the ancient sites lying around), the sandy beaches and warm Mediterranean make this one of the easiest and most appealing activities to fit into your trip. Some of the prettiest beaches are located along the far western coast (near Zuara) and in Cyrenaica, such as the seaside village of Ras al-Hammamah. You could also

choose to bring your swimwear on a visit to ancient sites such as Leptis Magna or Sabratha, for the added advantage of an amazing backdrop to your swim. However, the most memorable swimming spot in Libya has to be the desert lakes (*see pp110 & 120–21*). Admittedly, categorising this as swimming is a stretch, as the experience is more like flotation.

A cultural point to note is that the difference in clothing etiquette for men and women is really noticeable on beaches. If there are locals around, it is advisable for women to swim in shorts and a T-shirt. Even then, you may feel uncomfortable. The ideal solution is to swim at a deserted beach (not difficult to find) or in a desert lake. Men and children should be fine in normal swimwear.

Trekking

Trekking is one of a number of activities that could easily be accommodated by Libya's landscape, but it is little done at the moment. The hilly northern regions of the Jebel al-Akhdar and the Jebel Nafusa are particularly enticing as potential trekking destinations. While specific trekking tours and marked routes do not exist yet, it should be relatively straightforward to arrange with your tour company to have some hill walking included in your itinerary.

Water sports

Snorkelling and scuba diving along Libya's coast could be amazing, as some of the ancient sites include submerged ruins. However, there are no established companies or schools specialising in these activities, so arranging them can be complicated. Rules governing the protection of the ruins dictate that permission must be sought from the Department of Antiquities for any scuba diving. Your tour company may be able to arrange this for you, but there are no guarantees that permission will be granted. Arkno Tours (*see p130*) features a 'Diving and Cultural Tour', which includes boat and beach dives.

You don't need the white stuff to go skiing!

Children

In Libyan culture, children are welcomed and accepted pretty much everywhere, including restaurants. It is typical to see families with young children out and about until late in the evening. The downside is that the tourism industry in Libya is largely geared to adults. There are very few attractions designed for children, and keeping them entertained could be a challenge. There is plenty of scope, however, for imaginative and educational exploration of the fantastical desert landscapes and ruined sights.

Practicalities

Travelling around Libya, especially within the Sahara, often involves long, monotonous journeys. Bring plenty of things to keep your children entertained and pack a comprehensive first aid kit as pharmacies, although generally well stocked, are sparse in most of the country. The hot summer months are best avoided with young children; late autumn or early spring would be better choices.

Animals

As one of very few family attractions in Libya, **Tripoli Zoo** (*Open: 9am–5pm. Admission charge*) is popular with local families. The animals seem to be reasonably well cared for and have adequate space. Along with a number of non-native species such as elephants and lions, there are some desert animals like waddan and gazelles. The zoo is set in a large park called An-Nasr Forest, to the south of the city. **Fezzan Park** (*Tel/fax: (071) 632 860*), a camp near

Sebha, also has a small zoo with a collection of desert animals including ostriches, gazelles and reptiles. For a more hands-on experience, consider a camel ride. Although long tours on camel-back may be too much for children, a short ride in the desert can be an exciting activity. Your tour company may be able to arrange this during a visit to Ghadames or elsewhere in the desert.

Sea and sand

Libya has beaches, the Mediterranean Sea, incredible sand dunes and desert lakes. With these raw ingredients at your disposal, it should be possible to adapt a trip to be more child-friendly. One idea would be to pack a picnic and bring along the children's swimwear and beach toys when visiting coastal sites. Children can play at being desert explorers, climbing the dunes and seeing how salt-encrusted they end up after a dip in the lakes. The heat is a factor to take into consideration for desert trips, but in the winter it should be manageable. Camping in the Sahara is a memorable experience in itself for adults and children, especially when the night sky is clear enough to see the stars.

Sights

Most of Libya's top sights are fascinating enough to interest children as well as adults. The enchanting old city of Ghadames (*see pp86–91*), with its traditional houses, is particularly recommended for all ages. The Berber *qasrs* of the Jebel Nafusa, especially the labyrinthine qasr at Nalut (*see p93*), have a certain sci-fi appeal that should set young imaginations working. Gharyan's Berber houses (*see pp98–9*), the old bathhouses at Cyrene (*see pp68–9*) and the massive cisterns at Tolmeita (*see p77*) are all intriguing underground places. And children learning about Roman history might enjoy exploring Leptis Magna (*see pp48–55*) or visiting the theatre at Sabratha (*see p59*).

Short camel rides can be fun for children

Essentials

Arriving and departing

Libya has two main international airports, at Tripoli and Benghazi. Travellers also arrive and depart via the land borders with Tunisia and Egypt. There are no ferry services, but some cruises include stops in Libya. **Afriqiyah Airways** (*www.afriqiyah.aero*) and **British Airways** (*www. britishairways.com*) operate regular routes to Libya from the UK. There are direct flights with various airlines from other European countries and from Middle Eastern countries, and flights mainly with Afriqiyah from countries in Africa.

Customs

Customs checks on arrival focus mainly on alcohol. On departure, officials check for illegal souvenirs such as fragments of rock paintings. Bags are X-rayed and passports stamped several times, but the process tends to be quite fast-flowing.

Electricity

Plugs vary between the European two-pin type and the UK three-pin type. Appliances must take 220–240V AC.

Internet

Almost all Libyan towns have an Internet café and some hotels have Internet access, but Wi-Fi is uncommon.

Money

Libya's currency is the Libyan dinar (LD), which is divided into 100 piastres. You will mainly see notes, in denominations of 0.25, 0.5, 1, 5, 10 and 20 LD, although you may get some change in 0.25 and 0.5 LD coins. Dinars cannot be purchased or exchanged outside Libya so travellers should bring

Typical North African architecture in Tripoli

cash in euros, British pounds or US dollars to exchange on arrival. There is a bureau de change in the airport, and larger hotels have exchange counters or mini-branches of banks. Remember to change any leftover money back before leaving. Libya is a cash society and, although ATMs are becoming more widespread, the best approach is to exchange as much as you think you will need. Visa credit and debit cards are the most widely accepted variety in ATMs and banks. Crime rates are extremely low and carrying money should not be a problem as long as you take the usual precautions, such as wearing a secure belt. The Tuareg craftsmen of the desert widely accept euros, and foreign currency can also be used to pay for tours and in some shops in Tripoli.

Opening hours

Opening hours vary between types of establishment and may also vary seasonally. Many museums are only open in the morning and some are closed on certain days of the week. Shops tend to stay open into the evening but may close in the middle of the day for a siesta. Very few shops or businesses are open on Fridays. It is worth noting that although smaller or more remote tourist sites are sometimes unexpectedly closed, the person with the key can usually be found nearby.
Banks: *Sun–Tue & Thur 9am–1pm, Wed & Sat 8am–12.30pm & 3.30–4.30 or 5.30pm. Closed: Fri.*

CONVERSION TABLE

FROM	TO	MULTIPLY BY
Inches	Centimetres	2.54
Feet	Metres	0.3048
Yards	Metres	0.9144
Miles	Kilometres	1.6090
Acres	Hectares	0.4047
Gallons	Litres	4.5460
Ounces	Grams	28.35
Pounds	Grams	453.6
Pounds	Kilograms	0.4536
Tons	Tonnes	1.0160

To convert back, for example from centimetres to inches, divide by the number in the third column.

A marble frieze of Hercules at Leptis Magna

Essentials

Post offices and other government offices: *Sat or Sun–Thur 7am–2pm or 8am–3pm, depending on the time of year. Closed: Fri.*

Passports and visas

Unless you are a national of an African or Arab country, most of which are exempt from the following requirements, you will need a visa to enter Libya. The situation regarding visas has changed many times and may well have been altered again since the time of writing, so it is important to double-check.

To gain entry to Libya as a tourist, your visit must be arranged by a certified tour company. They basically 'invite' you to the country, organise your visa and agree to take responsibility for you during your stay. The company needs to be accredited in Libya, whether they are an entirely Libyan organisation or an international company with an affiliation. Once you have booked a tour, you will need to send a copy of your passport and flight details to the company. It is their responsibility to arrange your visa and send copies of the approval letter in Arabic, as well as a translation, to you and to the airline. Recently, the Libyan government added an extra biometric requirement to the visa application process. It stipulates that applicants must have their fingerprints taken at the Libyan People's Bureau before a visa will be issued.

Finally, you must get the details page of your passport translated into Arabic. This requirement has recently been strictly enforced and visitors without a certified translation have reported being turned away. You will need to arrange the Arabic passport translation yourself by contacting a translator (your tour company may be able to recommend someone) and getting a certified stamp from the passport office in your home country. The translator will write the translation onto the stamp.

Israeli citizens are not permitted to enter Libya at all, and visas will not be issued to anyone with an Israeli stamp in their passport. American citizens may also have difficulty obtaining visas, depending on the current political relationship between Libya and the USA.

Your tour company will arrange for your passport to be registered with the Libyan authorities when you arrive – a further requirement.

Pharmacies

Libyan pharmacies are well stocked and you should be able to find medication for any common minor illnesses, as well as general necessities like toiletries and sunscreen. Pharmacists can provide advice, but it is a good idea to ask your tour guide to accompany you in case translation is needed. Pharmacies are only found in major towns, so desert-trippers should be equipped with first aid kits.

Essentials

Post

Post offices, which are linked to telephone offices, can be found in most town centres. It is definitely best to go into a post office to send mail, rather than use postboxes (even if you do see one). The system is reliable, but post sent from smaller towns can take a lot longer to reach its destination than anything sent from the main post offices in Tripoli or Benghazi. Within Libya, post is delivered to post-office boxes, not to street addresses.

Public holidays

These dates are typically celebrated with speeches and rallies and most businesses close to mark the occasions. The Day of Mourning (26 October) is the main one to watch out for, as international communications are cut off for the day.
2 March (Declaration of the People's Authority Day, commemorating the establishment of the Jamahiriya)
28 March (Evacuation Day, commemorating the departure of British forces)
11 June (Evacuation Day, commemorating the departure of other foreigners who had air bases in Libya)
1 September (Revolution Day, also known as National Day)
26 October (Day of Mourning)

Smoking

Smoking is a popular habit in Libya and is allowed in almost all public places.

Suggested reading and media

Fiction

Anubis: A Desert Fable, Ibrahim al-Koni
The Bleeding of the Stone, Ibrahim al-Koni
In the Country of Men, Hisham Matar
Libyan Stories: Twelve Short Stories from Libya, (ed) Ahmed Ibrahim al-Fagih
The Seven Veils of Seth, Ibrahim al-Koni
The Shadows of Ghadames, Joelle Stolz

Non-fiction

African Rock Art: Paintings and Engravings on Stone, David Coulson and Alec Campbell
The Cambridge Illustrated History of the Islamic World, Ira M Lapidus and Francis Robinson
Kiss the Hand You Cannot Sever, Adrienne Brady
Libya: The Lost Cities of the Roman Empire, Robert Polidori, et al
Rome in Africa, Susan Raven
Sahara: A Natural History, Marc de Villiers and Sheila Hirtle
Unfolding Islam, P J Stewart

Media

There is only one English-language local newspaper, *The Tripoli Post*, which is produced fortnightly. It can be difficult to find and is obviously government controlled, as are Libyan TV and radio stations. Many hotels also have satellite TV with international channels.

Film and music

Lion of the Desert (1981)
Musiques du Sahara, by Tuareg de Fewet

Websites

Libyana Run by local volunteers
to share snapshots of Libyan culture,
such as traditional recipes, samples
of artwork and downloadable
music. *www.libyana.org*
Trust for African Rock Art
www.africanrockart.org

Tax

There is a small airport departure tax,
but this will in all probability be
included in the package with your tour
company. There is no value-added
tax (VAT).

Telephones

The country code for Libya is 218. If
dialling Libya from overseas, use the
country code followed by the area code
minus the initial 0. Mobile numbers
begin with 091 or 092. Although many
Libyans primarily use mobiles, there
is a reliable landline system for domestic
or international calls. Post offices
double as government telephone
offices, with phone booths. Go to the
counter with the number you want to
call and the clerk will connect the call.
After hanging up, go back to the
counter to pay. International phone
cards, which you can use at Internet
cafés, are also available. International
mobiles may or may not work.
Alternatively, if you make sure your
phone is unlocked before your trip,
you can pick up a pay-as-you-go
Libyan SIM card.

Time

Libya is two hours ahead of GMT,
although in the summer months
(March to October) the time difference
is reduced to one hour, as the clocks
are not adjusted for daylight saving
time in Libya.

Toilets

Libyan towns do not have public
toilets, but most tourist sites and
museums do. There is a minimal
charge occasionally, but the majority
are free and also clean, although toilet
paper is not always provided. It is a
good idea to bring packets of tissues
and a small bottle of alcohol hand gel
(particularly useful in the desert).
When in towns and cities, the best bet
is to ask to use the toilets at any
restaurant, tea house or hotel.
Ghadames is a notable exception, as
there are no toilets at all in the old
city. The closest public toilets are in
the museum.

Travellers with disabilities

An important consideration for
travellers with disabilities is to inform
your tour company of your specific
requirements as early as possible. They
can then help you plan the best
itinerary and make any necessary
adjustments. There are access issues to
some of the archaeological sites for
travellers with reduced mobility. Most
of the newer hotels have wide entrances
and lifts.

Read up on the Roman era before visiting the artefacts at Jamahiriya Museum

Language

The official language of Libya is Arabic. The Tuareg and Berber peoples speak their own languages as well as Arabic. Many of the Tuareg also speak French, due to links with Niger. English and other European languages (predominantly French or Italian) are spoken by people working in tourism, but are not widely learnt by Libyans in general. Learning some Arabic will certainly enrich your experience of travelling in Libya, although having a tour guide on hand to translate for you minimises language barrier problems.

Learning Arabic

The **British Council** has a new Libya office (*Tel: (218) 484 3164. www. britishcouncil.org/libya*). It is located outside Tripoli, off the road to Janzur. This is a good point of contact for Arabic language courses. If you just want to learn a few phrases, besides those listed here, pick up an Arabic phrase book. There are subtle differences in dialect across Libya and with neighbouring countries. However, thanks to the media, Libyans generally understand different varieties of Arabic, including those spoken in Egypt, Tunisia and Lebanon. If in doubt as to how to pronounce a phrase, ask your tour guide or driver how they would say it.

Useful phrases and common expressions

Salaam aleikum	literally 'peace be upon you', the most common form of greeting
Aleikum salam	response to greeting
Sabah alkheer	good morning
Sabah an-noor	response
Masa alkheer	good afternoon/evening
Masa an-noor	response
Ahlan	hello
Ahlan beek	response
Ahlan wa Sahlan	welcome
Ma salaama	literally 'peace be with you', goodbye
In sha Allah	literally 'God willing', a very common phrase used when talking of future events, could be translated as 'hopefully' or 'perhaps'

Aywa/na'am	yes
La	no
Min fadlak/birabbi	please
Shukran/barkalla oo feek	thank you
Saamah'nee	excuse me
Mitaasif/a	sorry, m/f
Ma feesh	'we haven't any' or 'there is none', a common phrase
Shi ismak?	what's your name?
Ismi…	my name is…
Giddash?	How much?
Wayn…?	where is…?
Inlowij'ala	I'm looking for
Funduq	hotel
Matam	restaurant

Written information

Due to the complicated process of transcribing words from one alphabet to another, you may well notice the same local words spelt in various different ways in the Roman alphabet. This is particularly true of names for people and places. For a start, common spellings of the Libyan leader's name include Qaddafi, Gaddafi and Qadhafi, among other variants. The many variably spelt place-names include the Acacus, which is sometimes written Akakus or Acacous.

Most road and business signs are written only in Arabic script. There are a few exceptions, such as the old street signs in Tripoli's medina, which are spelt out in the Roman alphabet as well. Numbers, on the other hand, generally appear in both Arabic and Western forms, so telephone numbers and distances at least can be read by non-Arabic speakers.

Signs for popular destinations

البيضاء	Al Bayda	صبراتة	Sabratha
بنغازي	Benghazi	سبها	Sebha
شحات	Cyrene (Shahat)	طبرق	Tobruk
غدامس	Ghadames	طرابلس	Tripoli (Tarabulus)
لبدة الكبرى	Leptis Magna	زوارة	Zuara
ليبيا	Libya		

Emergencies

Embassies and consulates

In the case of most emergencies, contact your embassy or consulate. The working week is from Sunday to Thursday and office hours are generally 8am–3 or 3.30pm. However, embassies also offer out-of-hours emergency contacts. One of the most commonly provided services is passport issuing. Practical help is available for various other emergencies, but financial help generally is not. For this you should contact your insurance company.

Australia *Office 203, Level 20, Tower 1, Burj al-Fateh, Tripoli.*
Tel: (021) 335 1468/69.
Fax: (021) 335 1368.
Email: eric.cantwell@austrade.gov.au
Canada *7th Floor, Tower 1, Burj al-Fateh, Tripoli (PO Box 93392).*
Tel: (021) 335 1633. Fax: (021) 335 1630.
Email: trpli@international.gc.ca
UK *24th floor, Burj al-Fateh, Tripoli (PO Box 4206). Tel: (021) 340 3644/5.*
Fax: (021) 335 1425.
Email: tripoliconsular@fco.gov.uk
USA *Serraj Area (connection street between Al Serraj and Al Krimia streets), Tripoli. Tel: 091 220 3239/0125 (out of hours).*
Email: tripoliconsular@state.gov.
http://libya.usembassy.gov

Emergency services

The emergency telephone numbers are *121* or *191*, but rescue services cannot be relied upon, especially in remote areas.

Health risks

One of the biggest health risks is heat-related illness. Make sure you protect yourself from the sun and drink plenty of fluids. It is important, for those travelling into the desert, to be as well prepared and self-sufficient (as a group) as possible. If you are injured or fall ill on a desert trip, assistance is unlikely to be quickly available.

Insurance

Comprehensive travel insurance is extremely important. Check that your policy would cover medical evacuation to your home country or to the nearest appropriate hospital if need be. This is likely to be necessary in the unfortunate case of a serious emergency, as local hospitals may be limited in their ability to provide more than immediate care.

Medical services

There is considerable variation in availability and standards of healthcare across Libya. There is a good range of medical facilities in Tripoli, including a couple of private clinics. The other cities and most towns also have hospitals, but those outside the main urban areas are unlikely to be very well equipped. You will have to pay for any medical treatment you require and claim on your

If you're travelling with a tour company, ground handlers will come to your rescue if needed

insurance later, but treatment is relatively inexpensive. Consult your doctor or tour company before travelling if you have an existing medical condition and bring any medication you may require. Glasses or contact lens wearers should bring spare pairs just in case. Avoid wearing lenses in the desert if possible, or at least take extra care, due to the combination of wind and sand.

Police, safety and crime

Libya is generally a very safe country to travel around. Crimes against tourists are incredibly rare, so the general precautions you would take anywhere should suffice. Tour groups of four or more are allocated a tourist police officer to accompany them. This is more part of the general bureaucracy than a reflection on safety. On desert trips, travel in a convoy of more than one vehicle and with a set of spare parts. Areas bordering Chad, Sudan, Niger and Algeria (with the exception of Ghadames and Ghat) are often unsafe. Check current advice.

Directory

Accommodation price guide

★	Under 30 LD
★★	31–60 LD
★★★	61–100 LD
★★★★	Over 100 LD

Prices are based on an average double room with bathroom unless otherwise specified.

It is worth noting that communications systems in much of Libya are not yet developed to the same level as in Tripoli. Street addresses are not given for a number of entries listed in this directory, simply because they are rarely used outside the main cities. Many hotels still do not have websites, although this is gradually changing. Telephone systems can be unreliable in remote areas, most notably Ghadames. Fortunately, as tour operators take care of the practicalities of making reservations and getting you to your hotel, these issues should not cause any inconvenience.

Eating out price guide

★	Under 10 LD
★★	10–15 LD
★★★	15–24 LD
★★★★	Over 24 LD

Prices are based on an average à la carte meal (which includes a main course with soup and/or salad) unless otherwise specified. Most restaurants are open 12.30–3pm for lunch and then 6.30–10pm for dinner. However, opening times are often quite flexible. Restaurants are typically closed during the day on Fridays, but usually open for dinner.

TRIPOLI
Medina and west of Al-Sada al-Khadra (Green Square)
ACCOMMODATION
A number of new private mid-range hotels have sprung up to the west of Green Square and the medina. Many of these are clustered in the same small network of streets north of Sharia Omar al-Mukhtar. The area in and around the medina is also where several of Tripoli's top hotels are located.

Al Okhowa Hotel ★★★
This is one of several shiny new hotels that have recently opened in the capital. Al Okhowa has bright modern décor and a good range of facilities, including wireless Internet, a café and restaurant, and laundry service.
Al Rafai (side street), *Sharia Omar al-Mukhtar.* *Tel: (021) 333 2191/1841/ 5946/1910/6222. Fax: (021) 444 9173.* *www.okhowahotel.com/en*

Funduq al-Andalus ★★★
This is one of several good-quality, reasonably priced hotels in this part of Tripoli. It has bright, well-equipped rooms with facilities including satellite TV.
Sharia al-Kindi. *Tel: (021) 334 3777.*

Al Waddan Hotel ★★★★

Built by the Italians in the 1930s, Al Waddan is Tripoli's oldest hotel and occupies an enviable city centre waterfront spot. The original building has been renovated by InterContinental Hotels and reopened in 2009 as a stylish boutique hotel. It combines period features such as courtyards with modern conveniences, including wireless Internet, satellite TV, and several cafés and restaurants.

Dahra, Tripoli.
Tel: (021) 333 0044.
Fax: (021) 333 0041.
www.alwaddanhotel.com

Corinthia Bab Africa Hotel ★★★★

Libya's only five-star hotel is absolutely in a league of its own. The elegant exterior and beautifully styled interior make staying here a visual treat as well as a luxurious and relaxing experience. The rooms are spacious and contain every comfort guests could possibly need. Each room is also a great work of design, with polished wooden furniture, a warm colour scheme, artistic flourishes and big windows that contribute to a bright and breezy atmosphere. Large, indulgent bathrooms round off the picture. There are fantastic views over the city from the higher levels. The extensive range of facilities includes indoor and outdoor swimming pools, a gym and a spa. The jewel in the crown has to be the selection of restaurants (*see p163*). Try to spend a night here if you can, especially if returning from a desert trip, when you will particularly appreciate the food, the swimming pools and the all-round luxury.

Souq Al Thulatha,
Al Gadim.
Tel: (021) 335 1992.
www.corinthiahotels.com

Four Seasons Hotel ★★★★

Note that this is not part of the international Four Seasons chain; instead, it is quite uniquely Libyan in character. From the reception area to the rooms, everything is spacious and grandly decorated and there is a warm, welcoming atmosphere about the place. Internet connections in the rooms are among the comprehensive facilities. There is a café, and a restaurant serving Libyan and international dishes.

Sharia Omar al-Mukhtar.
Tel: (021) 333 2151.
Fax: (021) 334 0164.
www.fourseasons.com/ly

Thobacts Hotel ★★★★

This is another of Tripoli's new modern hotels. The facilities include accessible rooms for guests with disabilities, wireless Internet access and satellite TV. At the time of writing, there were plans to add a fitness centre and a roof terrace café. The hotel is in the top-end price bracket, but it advertises special offers that bring the rates down.

Sharia Omar al-Mukhtar.
Tel: (021) 334 4519.
Fax: (021) 334 4518.
www.hotel-thobacts.ly

Zumit Hotel ★★★★

Housed in one of the most faithfully restored buildings in the medina, the Zumit Hotel is

enchanting. A wonderful level of attention to detail, encompassing curved brick ceilings, mosaics, colourful rugs and lamps, has created plenty of atmosphere and, with the Arch of Marcus Aurelius practically on the doorstep, the location is perfect. At the centre of the hotel is a traditional courtyard, where meals and tea are served. Rooms branch off from a balcony overlooking the courtyard. Non-guests can also visit the building and eat at the restaurant. *Marcus Aurelius Arch Square.*
Tel: (021) 334 2915/ 444 6323/334 4102.
www.zumithotel.com

EATING OUT
Abiya (or Obaya) ★
Abiya is a great-value, cosy lunchtime haven in the heart of the old city. The chef serves up delicious dishes reminiscent of home-cooking in a first-floor dining room with windows overlooking one of the main streets of the medina. The seafood is fantastic and other choices include fish, couscous or macaroni. *Souq al-Turk No 144.*
Tel: 092 501 0736.
Open: lunch Sat–Thur.
Al Medina al-Kadima ★
There is a tea room downstairs and a restaurant upstairs in this traditional-style medina building. While the restaurant is a good bet for hearty typical dishes, the tea house is especially inviting because of its cheerful ambience. *Souq al-Turk.*
Tel: 092 688 9395.
Open: Sat–Thur 8.30am–11pm.
Magha as-Sa'a ★
This traditional tea house is located opposite the Ottoman clock tower in the medina, making it a perfect place to stop off after a day spent wandering in the souks. It is understandably popular and always busy and friendly. The outside tables are a great location for watching the world go by, while the inside rooms boast clock tower views (from upstairs) and quirky furnishings (downstairs). *Maidan al-Sa'a, Medina.*
Tel: 092 503 2510.
Open: 7am–2am.
Oriental Corner ★
This café and patisserie is sure to delight anyone with a sweet tooth, as well as coffee lovers. It is one of the few places in Tripoli where proper cappuccinos are served, but the real draw is the vast selection of sweets and little cakes made with nuts and honey. *Ben Ashoor Street.*
Tel: (021) 360 5320/ 360 9232.
Al-Bourai ★★
This is another appealing medina restaurant, where dishes are traditional but inventive. *Sharia Jama ad-Draghut.*
Tel: 092 716 6560.
Open: lunch Sat–Thur.
Athar Restaurant ★★★
With a wide balcony seating area arranged in a horseshoe around the Arch of Marcus Aurelius, the view from this restaurant is unique. It is particularly special in the evening, when the arch is illuminated and a band plays live music. Although the setting is

really the star attraction, the traditional Libyan food is also great. The *algarra* (*see p136*) is a speciality, and having your dish broken out of an amphora at your table adds to the experience. All the dishes, from the soups and salads to the meat and fish dishes, are very well-prepared versions of the classics. Athar is part of the Ghazala group, which runs two other restaurants in Tripoli.
Arch of Marcus Aurelius, the old city sea gate.
Tel: (021) 444 7001.
Email:
info@ghazalagroup.com.
www.ghazalagroup.com.
Open: lunch & dinner.

Essaa ★★★
Next to the Ottoman clock tower, this pleasant and atmospheric restaurant offers a traditional experience complete with live music and the typical banquet-style meals. The restaurant is upstairs, overlooking the little square in front of the clock tower, while coffee and tea are served in the coffee house on the

ground floor. This is a classic set-up, which you may come across in several medina restaurants.
Tel: 091 219 0683.
Open: Sat–Thur lunch & dinner, Fri dinner.

Tripolis ★★★
This restaurant has a prime location across the road from the harbour, just outside the medina. It is on the first floor of an impressive building, which doubles as an arts and crafts centre during the day. Tastefully decorated, with wood beams, ornamental lights and big windows, this is a charming place for an evening meal. They have a menu in English and vegetarian options.
Sharia Jama ad-Draghut (next to Central Bank of Libya on outskirts of medina).
Tel: (021) 444 8859/ 092 558 0817.

Corinthia Bab Africa Hotel restaurants ★★★★
For a change from the typical Libyan fare, the restaurants of the Corinthia Hotel offer plenty of variety. There is a choice of Moroccan,

Italian, Chinese, outdoor grills on the terrace and extensive buffets. The standard of food and design is high in all the restaurants. Fez Moroccan Restaurant, on the top floor, has romantic mood lighting and stunning views over the city. Meanwhile, the Terrace Restaurant has a refreshing roof garden party feel to it and Venezia Italian Restaurant is decidedly classy.
Souq Al Thulatha, Al Gadim.
Tel: (021) 335 1992.
www.corinthiahotels.com

ENTERTAINMENT
Hammams (Turkish baths) are popular places for socialising. In the steam rooms, massages and body scrubs are on offer at minimal prices.

Hammam al-Heyga
Trigh al-Heygha.
Open: 8am–3pm (women: Mon, Thur, Sat & Sun; men: Tue, Wed & Fri).

Hammam al-Kebira
Sharia Homet Gharyan.
Open: 8am–3pm

(women: Mon–Wed; men: Thur–Sun).

Hammam Draghut
Souq al-Turk. Open: 8am–3pm (women: Mon–Wed; men: Thur–Sun).

East of Al-Sada al-Khadra (Green Square)
ACCOMMODATION

Buyut ash-Shabaab ★
This youth hostel has extremely low prices and a great central location to recommend it, but it is very rustic. There are shared bathrooms and basic meals are available. If you are thinking of staying in hostels elsewhere in Libya, this is the place to come for information (*see p135*).
Sharia A ibn al-Ass. Tel/fax: (021) 333 0118.

Funduq Gharnata ★★
This is one of Tripoli's cheaper mid-range hotels and offers a reasonable standard in a good location.
Sharia al-Baladiya. Tel: (021) 444 0647. Fax: (021) 333 6054.

Al Kebir Hotel ★★★
This government-run hotel is one of the longest-established hotels in Tripoli and it has quite an old-fashioned vibe. It has a very convenient location right in the city centre. The facilities include a fitness centre, swimming pool and bank.
Sharia Al-Fatah. Tel: (021) 444 5940/58. Fax: (021) 333 1762. Email: alkebir-hotel@lttnet.net

Dar Arkno Guest House ★★★
This villa succeeds in creating a welcoming home-style impression. There are just seven guest rooms, plus a traditional lounge and dining room. The rooms and bathrooms are spacious and tastefully decorated. Located in a quiet part of the city, it also has a lovely little courtyard garden.
Arkno Tours. Tel: (021) 444 4044. Email: info@arkno.com. www.arkno.com

Funduq Attawfeek ★★★
Located in a quiet area to the east of Algeria Square, this is a comfortable option with sizeable rooms, balconies, Internet access and buffet breakfasts.
Sharia Qusban. Tel: (021) 444 7253.

Funduq al-Mehari ★★★★
At the time of writing, the Mehari, one of Tripoli's longest-standing top-end hotels, had just closed for renovations. It is included here because it was one of the most attractive of the government-owned hotels. Highlights included friendly staff, extensive buffet breakfasts and fantastic views over the city from the higher levels. It was also quite popular with tour companies and will be again when it reopens in 2010.
Sharia al-Fat'h. Tel: (021) 333 4091/6. Fax: (021) 444 9502.

EATING OUT

In addition to the places below, there are tea houses around the perimeter of Green Square, and Matam al-Saraya (*see below*) is also popular for evening tea-drinking.

Gazelle Café ★
A garden-style café, this is located by a distinctive fountain between Algeria Square and the parkland. The usual choice of teas

and coffee are on offer.
No telephone.

Maidan al-Jezayir tea houses ★

On the north side of Algeria Square, next to the post office, a couple of small tea houses set up outdoor tables on a terraced area. This is an attractive spot to have tea, with whitewashed arches overhead, parkland to the north and the stunning Jamal Abdel Nasser Mosque just across the square.
No telephone.

Barakoda Restaurant ★★

Located in the fish market, this restaurant makes the most of its seaside atmosphere with a decked outdoor seating area that literally overlooks the waterfront. You can choose your own fish from the market and the kitchen will prepare it for you. They also do a range of salads.
Fish market (road between Tripoli & Tajura). Tel: 091 320 6971/ 092 515 3796.

Matam al-Saraya Café ★★

The café attached to the restaurant of the same name is great for a laidback lunch, which can be enjoyed in the garden, surrounded by the palm trees and sea breezes of Tripoli's waterfront. There is a good choice of casual lunch options, such as sandwiches, pizza and salads, and the garden also serves as a popular tea garden in the evening.
Al-Sada al-Khadra (Green Square). Tel: (021) 333 4433. Open: noon–1am.

Matam as-Safir ★★

This excellent-value restaurant oozes traditional style, from the unpretentious tasty food to the décor. The dining room is traditionally styled with high-arched ceilings and patterned mosaic tiles on the walls. A warm ambience is created by soft lighting and traditional music. The service is friendly and English is spoken.
Sharia al-Baladia (behind the Grand Hotel). Tel: (021) 444 7064/ 091 213 7359. Open: Sat–Thur lunch & dinner, Fri dinner.

Galaxie Restaurant ★★★

A hidden gem above a snack bar, Galaxie's restaurant section serves satisfying portions of high-quality food. The menu, available in English, includes fantastic internationally inspired salads, mixed grills and vegetarian options.
Sharia 1 September. Tel: (021) 444 8764. Open: lunch & dinner.

Kenouz al-Bahar Restaurant ★★★

This classy restaurant specialises in fish, seafood and lamb dishes, many of which are Tunisian-style. The service is welcoming and the restaurant in general is an inviting and leisurely place to linger over a meal. It is open for lunch and dinner, but its location right on the atmospheric Algeria Square makes it a particularly good evening choice.
Maidan al-Jezayir (Algeria Square). Tel: (021) 333 4321/ 092 506 0567.

Al-Saraya restaurant ★★★★

The upstairs restaurant attached to the café of the same name is fancier and more suited to an

evening meal. There is a mixture of Libyan and Lebanese cuisine and a range of set menus.
Al-Sada al-Khadra (Green Square).
Tel: (021) 333 4433.
Open: noon–1am.

Ghazalet Afriqia ★★★★
Tucked away down a back street, this classy restaurant is a great find. It is part of the Ghazala group, along with Athar and Shera'a restaurants. The menu is varied and includes a selection of soups, salads, pasta, fish and meat dishes and desserts. In the evenings, there is a salad buffet to start. There is live music some nights.
Aldhahra.
Tel: (021) 444 7000.
Email:
info@ghazalagroup.com.
www.ghazalagroup.com.
Open: lunch & dinner.

Shera'a Restaurant ★★★★
Another offering of the upmarket Ghazala group, this large seafront restaurant has formal décor but friendly atmosphere. The menu is much the same as at Ghazalet Afriqia, and there is live music on

offer some evenings.
Alshat Alkadim Road, by the Italian Embassy.
Tel: (021) 712 2534.
Email:
info@ghazalagroup.com.
www.ghazalagroup.com.
Open: lunch & dinner.

TRIPOLITANIA: LEPTIS MAGNA AND SABRATHA
East (around Leptis Magna)
ACCOMMODATION
Al-Madinah Hotel ★
This good-value hotel is one of the best places to stay in the vicinity of Leptis Magna. Rooms have en-suite bathrooms, TV and air conditioning.
Al Khums.
Tel: (031) 620 799.

Leptes Hotel ★
This is another decent, well-priced hotel near the ancient site, with similar facilities to the Al-Madinah.
Al Khums.
Tel: (031) 621 252.

Severus Hotel ★★★
At just 4km (2½ miles) from Leptis Magna, this smart hotel in the coastal town of Al Khums is a convenient base for

exploring the ancient site and the region.
Al-Fatah Street, Al Khums.
Tel: (031) 262 5086/7.
Fax: (031) 262 5089.
Email: info@severus.ly

EATING OUT
Matam al-Khayma ★
Both this restaurant and Matam al-Najar (*see below*) are roadside eateries reputed for their local specialities.
Near Al Khums (13km/ 8 miles along the road to Tripoli).
Tel: 091 320 5169.

Matam al-Najar ★
*Same as Matam al-Khayma (*see above*).*
Tel: 091 320 5398.

Tourist restaurant, Leptis Magna ★★★
Popular with tour groups, this place has a bright, welcoming vibe and serves up hearty portions of hot food. It makes a good alternative to the snack options on the site.
Opposite Car Park No 1 on the road in from Tripoli.

West (around Sabratha)
ACCOMMODATION
Funduq al-Asil ★★
There are not many accommodation options

around Sabratha, but this hotel is reasonably priced and well equipped.
Sabratha.
Tel: (025) 220 553.

Farah Resort ★★★
This seaside tourist village located just west of Zuara has several bonuses that are still unusual in the Libyan accommodation scene. For a start, it is family-centred, with suites and large villas. In addition, there is a swimming pool, and various activities are available or planned. The price code is based on dividing the rate for a villa.
Zuara. Tel: (025) 220 542.

Dar Tellile ★★★★
This new luxury all-inclusive resort is the most upmarket accommodation in the area. It is hidden away within a walled compound and could be more outwardly welcoming. However, the building is elegant and the resort has a wealth of facilities, including swimming pools.
Near Sabratha.
Tel: (024) 643 030/11.
Fax: (024) 643 006.

EATING OUT
Matam al-Bawady ★★
There are not many good places to eat around Sabratha, so this restaurant stands out for its high-quality food and service.
Sabratha.
Tel: (024) 620 224.
Open: lunch & dinner.

CYRENAICA
Benghazi
ACCOMMODATION
El-Fadeel Hotel ★★
The list of amenities at this hotel is quite extensive for the price category. Balconies attached to each room, an Internet café (and individual computers in the suites), laundry service and restaurants are among the selling points.
Sharia el-Shatt.
Tel: (061) 909 9795. Email: elfadeelhotel@hotmail.com

Qaryat Qar Yunis as-Siyahe (Tourist Village) ★★
One of the crop of popular tourist villages popping up along the coast, this is a vast complex with a choice of accommodation from single hotel rooms to

family-size apartments and villas. The guests, as at other tourist villages, are mainly local families and the prices are relatively low.
Sharia Qar Yunis, 6km (3³/₄ miles) south of Benghazi.
Tel: (061) 909 6903.

Tibesty Hotel ★★★★
This is one of Benghazi's premier hotels, equipped with an extensive range of facilities, including a health club and business centre. The rooms are well appointed and some have great views over the double harbour. The buffet breakfast spreads are varied and there is a choice of restaurants and cafés. The Italian restaurant is cosy and makes a change from Benghazi's Turkish and Arabic restaurants.
Sharia Jamal Abdel Nasser, Benghazi.
Tel: (061) 909 7160.
Fax: (061) 909 4477.
www.tebistyhotel.com

EATING OUT
A number of Benghazi's restaurants are concentrated in the area to the south of the old

city around Sharia Jamal Abdel Nasser, with a few across the 23 July Lake on Sharia Gulf of Sirt.

Souq al-Jreed ★
There is a drink stand in the Souq al-Jreed that serves fresh juices and milkshakes. When it comes to snacks, there is plenty of choice in Benghazi, including a falafel stall in Souq al-Jreed.

Matam Turki ★★
For a great-value, interesting, casual lunch, head to this gem of a Turkish restaurant. They serve up pizzas and mixed grills in huge portions or, for something lighter, a varied salad bar and delicious cheese bread. In the evening, they do traditional Turkish dishes such as *schwarma*.
Sharia 23 July.
Tel: (061) 909 1331.
Open: 10am–1am.

Matam al-Arabi ★★★
This popular Arabic restaurant provides a charming dining experience. The decoration is beautiful, the ambience has a soft glow and the meals are varied

and generous enough to really linger over.
Sharia Gulf of Sirt.
Tel: (061) 909 4468.
Open: Sat–Thur lunch & dinner, Fri dinner.

Matam Gharnata ★★★
This is a good solid choice for traditional multi-course Libyan meals.
Sharia Jamal Abdel Nasser.
Tel: (061) 909 3509.
Open: lunch & dinner.

Northern Cyrenaica
ACCOMMODATION
Cyrene Resort ★★
Located in a quiet area near Cyrene, this hotel has a serene garden setting. The rooms are basic but comfortable. Making good use of the geography of the area, the attached restaurant and café are set inside caves in the rock. There are also some alfresco tables.
Shahat village (near police station).
Tel/fax: (085) 164 391.

Loaloat al-Khalij Hotel ★★
This large hotel is one of the best options in Al Bayda. Besides the

standard rooms, which are a good size, there are also family and saloon suites. The lobby area, decorated with artworks, includes a coffee lounge and restaurant. The only potential downside at the time of writing was a problem with lift maintenance, but overall it is a good package.
Sharia al-Ruba, Al Bayda.
Tel: (084) 463 1979.
Fax: (084) 631 981.

Loaloat el-Jebel el-Akhdar Hotel ★★
At the lower end of the mid-range price scale, this hotel in the centre of Al Bayda is good value and well located. The rooms are nice, the service is attentive and all the expected facilities are included.
Sharia El Oroba (next to Internet café), Al Bayda.
Tel: (084) 630 968/70.
Fax: (084) 630 971.

El Manara Hotel ★★★
This is essentially the only place to stay near Apollonia. Luckily, it is superb. The ancient ruins are literally just down the road and there are also lovely sea views from some of the

rooms. The rooms themselves are attractive and comfortable, with balconies and good bathrooms. There is a decent restaurant that alternates between buffets and set meals.
Sousa (PO Box 999). Tel: (084) 515 3001/6.

EATING OUT
Asservium ★★
This is one of several good restaurants along Sharia al Ruba, which is the main eating district in Al-Bayda. Asservium stands out because of its terrace seating and vibrant atmosphere.
Sharia al-Ruba, Al Bayda. Open: Sat–Thur lunch & dinner, Fri dinner.

Barqa Restaurant ★★
Located in the pine forest at Cyrene, near the Temple of Zeus, this is an appealing little restaurant. They do traditional several-course meals to a good standard, which sets them apart from the more casual snack-bars nearer the main site.
Cyrene. Tel: 092 622 4490. Open: lunch & dinner.

Cave Restaurant ★★★
Carved into a rock face, the literally named Cave Restaurant is cosy and full of character. Warm lighting, tables nestled into rocky alcoves and good food add up to romantic potential. Located in the village of Shahat just outside Cyrene, it also makes a good lunch destination if you are looking for something a little different from the eateries inside the site.
Shahat, Cyrene. Tel: (085) 635 206.

Eastern Cyrenaica
ACCOMMODATION
Jaghboub Hotel ★★
Near the centre of the town, this bright, clean private hotel is one of the best in Tobruk. The staff are friendly and attentive. The breakfasts (included), TV and Internet access also add to the comfort rating. Rooms with en-suites and balconies cost extra.
Sharia al Jamahiriya, Tobruk. Tel: (087) 762 8260/092 569 5214.

EATING OUT
Matam al-Khalij ★★
This is arguably the top restaurant in Tobruk. It is housed in an easily spotted orange building and has a bright and breezy air. The harbour views contribute to a seaside vibe that will show you a lighter side to this serious town. One of the highlights of the bargain menu is the pizza, cooked in a traditional brick oven. Visitors also come to enjoy huge salads and mixed grilled fish.
Sharia al-Jamahiriya, Tobruk. Tel: 092 578 5344. Open: lunch & dinner.

JEBEL NAFUSA AND GHADAMES
Ghadames
ACCOMMODATION
Jawharat as-Sahra Hotel ★
This is more like a hostel than a hotel, with very cheap four-bed rooms. It is very close to the Bab al-Burr old city entrance and has a decent restaurant attached (*see p171*).
Tel/fax: (0484) 62 015.

Ben Yedder Hotel ★★
This hotel is also good

value and fairly new. The main added bonus is that it has a convenient location right in the centre of the modern town. With welcoming staff and nice bedrooms and bathrooms, this is a good option all-round.
Tel: (047) 786 3411/ 091 365 0193. Email: yedder@hotmail.com

Kasser el-Deawan Hotel ★★
This new hotel is located in a quiet area on the southern outskirts of Ghadames. The comfortable rooms are laid out like mini-suites, with little entrance-cum-sitting rooms (complete with satellite TV), as well as en-suite bathrooms and balconies.
Communal areas include a restaurant and a TV lounge on the landing. Friendly service completes the picture.
Tel: 091 363 9987/092 526 2188. Fax: (041) 361 5269.

Villa Abdealmoula ★★
This is one of a number of 'villas' in Ghadames. They are basically private homes with some guest rooms, run on a B&B

basis. This is a good unpretentious option, with a home-from-home vibe. Cooking facilities are usually available too.
Tel: (0484) 62 844. Email: villa_moula@yahoo.com

Winzrik Hotel ★★
This is a decent hotel in its price range. It also allows camping in the grounds. Campers will benefit from being on a secure site and having access to bathroom facilities.
Tel/fax: (0484) 62 485.

Kafila Hotel ★★★
This is one of the oldest hotels in Ghadames. The rooms are basic but spacious. Bookings are made through the Tripoli office.
Tel: (021) 360 9990. Email: kafilahotel1969@ hotmail.com

Dar Ghadames Hotel ★★★★
Easily the classiest accommodation in Ghadames, the beauty of this new hotel lies in its traditional design, which is perfectly in keeping with the spirit of the old city. The white building is surrounded by a landscaped garden, and

many of the rooms have terraces facing the cool greenery. The entrance hall is palatial, with chandeliers and arched columns, but in a bright minimalist way. Everything is painted white, and the winding corridors are particularly reminiscent of the old city. The rooms are both elegant and cosy. Carefully designed soft lighting emphasises the warm colour scheme of the traditional red bedspreads, rugs and cushions. There is a restaurant that serves inventive top-quality buffets, a tea house and a stylish lounge, with dance performances on some nights. Bookings are made through the Tripoli office.
Tel: (021) 363 9966. Fax: (0484) 63 408. www.darsahara.com

EATING OUT
There are only a few designated restaurants in Ghadames. However, all the hotels serve meals, and a number of the traditional houses serve lunch during the tourist

high season. Note that Ghadames is a very seasonal town and options can be even more limited outside the tourist high season.

Tiylooan ★

One of a few traditional-styled tea houses in the old city, with tables set out in a courtyard.
Northwest of Intelewan Square.

Tojada ★

This inviting little café is another good place to pick up some refreshments in the heart of the old city. It has a charming garden setting and laidback seating area with souvenirs on sale. Tea is served in traditional silver tea sets and accompanied by peanuts.
Off the street linking Tingazin Square & Intelewan Square.

Awwal Restaurant ★★

This little restaurant serves classic, well-made dishes and is a perennial favourite with travellers.
Next to the Internet café near the entrance to the old city. Tel: (0484) 62 429. Open: lunch & dinner.

Jawharat as-Sahra Restaurant ★★

Attached to the budget hotel (*see p169*), this casual restaurant is a good place to have something different from the set meals offered by the hotels.
Next to the Internet café near the entrance to the old city. Tel: (0484) 62 015. Open: Sat–Thur lunch & dinner, Fri dinner.

Jebel Nafusa
ACCOMMODATION
Dar Gharyan Hotel ★★

Given that visitors to Gharyan are hardly spoilt for choice in terms of accommodation, the Dar Gharyan is a reasonable option. The rooms are spacious, the price is fair and there is a buffet restaurant. It is located on the approach to town (Tripoli direction), just off the main road.
Gharyan. Tel: (041) 263 1482.

Rabta Hotel ★★

Although government-run, this is comparable to the Dar Gharyan in most respects. The rooms and the restaurant are reasonable enough.

Sharia al-Jamahiriya, Gharyan. Tel: (041) 631 970.

Winzrik Hotel ★★

Known as the 'ice cream hotel' because of its pastel Neapolitan colours, the Winzrik has a unique, if somewhat kitsch, character. The interior design may not be particularly inspiring, but the location makes up for this. The hotel is perched on a hill top overlooking the *qasr* of Nalut and the surrounding plains, so there are great views from the balcony.
Tel: (0470) 2204.

Yefren Hotel ★★

This is another well-situated Jebel Nafusa hotel, with panoramic views over the plain. The hotel has an elegant, nicely styled exterior and the interior is also appealing, with large, comfort-focused rooms.
Tel: (0421) 60 278.

EATING OUT
Ajweiba restaurant ★★

Located at a petrol station, this restaurant is very appealing in the middle of a long drive.

Its hearty home-cooking, cool dining room and friendly service are just what travellers need.

At the crossroads of the roads to Nalut & Gharyan/Ghadames. Tel: 092 679 8452/ 091 370 5327. Open: lunch & dinner.

Hanibal ★★

This is the only restaurant in Kabaw, so luckily it is a nice welcoming place and serves appetising dishes. It is ideally situated for a refreshment break during tours of the Jebel Nafusa.

Kabaw. Tel: (021) 487 3796. www.kabaw.com.ly. Open: lunch & dinner.

FEZZAN AND SAHARA

Accommodation and restaurant options are limited in this region.

Jebel Acacus

ACCOMMODATION AND EATING OUT

Acacus Magic Lodge ★★★★

The set-up here is the same as at the Ubari lodge (*see below*), but with a different backdrop.

The camp is located in a particularly scenic part of the Acacus and there are fantastic views from the tall rocks that encircle it.

Magic Libya Incoming & Tours, Libya Head Office, Tripoli. Tel: (021) 3408 355/732/ 731. Fax: (021) 340 8355. Email: info@ magic-dmc.com

Idehan Ubari

ACCOMMODATION AND EATING OUT

Ubari Magic Lodge ★★★★

The tour company Magic Libya have a semi-permanent desert camp near the Ubari lakes. Nestling among the dunes, the raised tents that make up the camp blend well with the scenery. Each tent includes a spacious sleeping area and a little bathroom. There are also large communal tents, one of which is set up for dining, while the other is scattered with rugs and cushions for relaxing in the evenings. This is a perfect solution for travellers who want to wake up surrounded by sand dunes, without giving up creature comforts.

Magic Libya Incoming & Tours, Libya Head Office, Tripoli. Tel: (021) 3408 355/732/731. Fax: (021) 340 8355. Email: info@ magic-dmc.com

Ghat

ACCOMMODATION

Acacous Tourist Hotel ★

This hotel near the medina in Ghat is basically the only place to stay in town, with the exception of a couple of camps. It is a decent hotel for the price bracket.

Ghat. Tel: (0724) 710 2769. Email: hotelacacousghat@ ghat.gov.ly

Germa area

ACCOMMODATION AND EATING OUT

Wat Wat Camping ★

This budget choice has basic huts but a nice shady outdoor eating area and a surprisingly lush landscaped garden. You can camp here or just stop off for a meal.

Between Germa and Ubari, just south of the highway. Tel: (0729) 642 471.

Funduq Dar Germa ★★
Dar Germa stands out for being a comfortable hotel with great facilities in an area mostly dominated by campsites. The décor is traditional and tasteful and all the rooms have en-suite bathrooms. There is a restaurant, cosy tea lounge, gift shop and a terrace with flowering plants.
Germa (Tripoli-Ghat road). Tel: (0729) 642 276. www.darsahara.com

Old City Tourist Restaurant ★★
This is a rustic restaurant which doubles as a campsite, with a kitchen for self-catering use.
Site entrance, Old Garama, Germa.

Sebha area
ACCOMMODATION
Fezzan Park ★–★★
This camp has a choice of cheap huts with communal bathrooms, or more comfortable suites. Breakfast is offered for a small additional charge. There is also a swimming pool and a zoo (*see p148*) on the site, with desert animals such as gazelles

and ostriches. Overall, this is one of the most interesting and popular places in the area.
Sharia al-Jamahiriya, about 10km (6 miles) out of Sebha, off the road to Ubari. Tel: (071) 632 860/092 513 1967.

Al-Waha Hotel ★★★
Offering the highest-quality accommodation in Sebha, this popular, shiny new hotel has fully equipped rooms and bathrooms. Breakfast is included in the room rates and there is a restaurant serving lunch and dinner.
Trih al-Tarablus al-Katib, Sebha. Tel: (071) 636 424. Email: alwaha_hotel@ yahoo.com

EATING OUT
Matam Acacus ★★
One of very few decent restaurants in Sebha, this is an understandable favourite with tour groups. The typical dishes are done reliably well and the atmosphere is inviting.
Sharia Mohammed Megharief, Sebha. Tel: (071) 634 934. Open: lunch & dinner.

Matam an-Nasser ★★
This is another popular choice with travellers. It tends to stay open quite late and has a casual vibe. There are two floors of seating: upstairs is for sit-down meals, while downstairs is more for snacks, drinks and sweets. The food is good, although not remarkable.
Sharia Jamal Abdel Nasser, Sebha. Tel: (071) 628 220. Open: lunch & dinner.

Al Aweinat
ACCOMMODATION AND EATING OUT
Alfaw Camp ★
This is a typical permanent desert camp, with thatched hut accommodation. There is a travel agency and also a restaurant serving up rustic fare on the site. Being located at the gateway to the Acacus, it is a bustling site and also one of the only places in the region in which to sleep and eat.
Al Aweinat. Tel/fax: (021) 334 0770. Email: alfawtravel@ yahoo.com

Index